Drive and Stroll in

Lancashire

Ron Freethy

COUNTRYSIDE BOOKS
NEWBURY BERKSHIRE

First published 2004
© Ron Freethy 2004

COUNTRYSIDE BOOKS
3 Catherine Road
Newbury, Berkshire

To view our complete range of books,
please visit us at
www.countrysidebooks.co.uk

ISBN 1 85306 841 1

Photographs by the author
Designed by Peter Davies, Nautilus Design

Produced through MRM Associates Ltd., Reading
Typeset by Techniset Typesetters, Newton-le-Willows
Printed by Woolnough Bookbinding Ltd., Irthlingborough

Contents

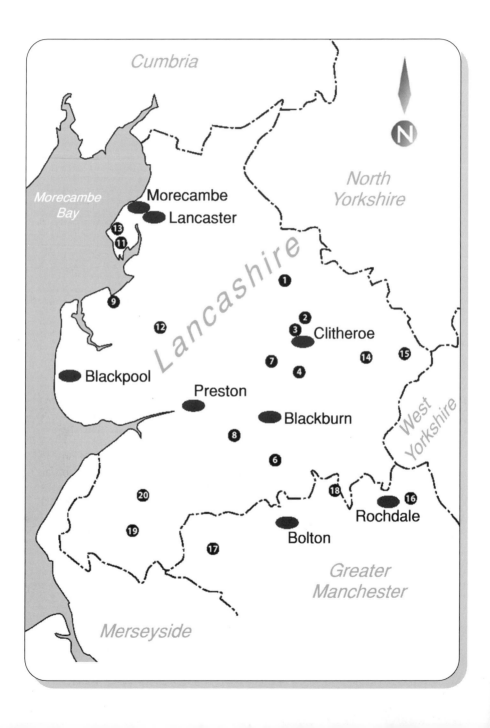

Contents

PUBLISHER'S NOTE

We hope that you obtain considerable enjoyment from this book; great care has been taken in its preparation. Although at the time of publication all routes followed public rights of way or permitted paths, diversion orders can be made and permissions withdrawn.

We cannot, of course, be held responsible for such diversion orders and any inaccuracies in the text which result from these or any other changes to the routes nor any damage which might result from walkers trespassing on private property. We are anxious though that all details covering the walks are kept up to date and would therefore welcome information from readers which would be relevant to future editions.

The simple sketch maps that accompany the walks in this book are based on notes made by the author whilst checking out the routes on the ground. They are designed to show you how to reach the start, to point out the main features of the overall circuit and they contain a progression of numbers that relate to the paragraphs of the text.

However, for the benefit of a proper map, we do recommend that you purchase the relevant Ordnance Survey sheet covering your walk. The Ordnance Survey maps are widely available, especially through booksellers and local newsagents.

Introduction

Way back in 1970 I was asked by the editor of the *Lancashire Evening Telegraph*, based in Blackburn, to write a weekly column, which was first called 'Freethy's England' and later 'Drive and Stroll'. I was a Lake District lad who had also spent many happy hours walking and photographing in the Yorkshire and Derbyshire Dales, and these areas were the subject of my articles, but it was not long before my readers were pointing out that there were also many beautiful drives and strolls in Lancashire. They were right!

Lancashire is the proud possessor of a landscape of majestic and breathtaking natural beauty, and over the last quarter of a century I have noticed that the dark satanic mills (not that they they were ever as dark or satanic as many writers have suggested) and other unfortunate man-made additions and modifications have gone and the hills and rivers have recovered from water and atmospheric pollution. Another change for the better has been the more enlightened attitude of landowners and local councils with regard to rights of way and footpath markings. The local water company (United Utilities) has been in the vanguard of improving access, while the National Trust is also encouraging walkers and publishing information leaflets.

Physical exercise, however leisurely, tends to generate an appetite and a thirst. The idea of a pie and a pint does not make sense these days in view of the drink-drive laws. There is nothing better than to enjoy a snack or a meal along with a soft drink or a cup of tea before, during, or after a stroll. This is the perfect way to fight the flab, and each walk focuses on a pub, cafe, or restaurant. Happily it is no longer considered odd to enter a pub and ask for a coffee!

Where relevant, I have indicated areas with picnic tables. We should all ensure that litter is disposed of properly. A picnic bag is always lighter at the end of the day and so any rubbish should be taken home. Dog lovers should also remember to take a supply of doggie 'poo bags'.

Maps are important to walkers, and the relevant maps and grid references have been listed for each walk. Quite rightly 'serious' walkers will plan their own much longer routes. Strollers, however, want literally to stroll and the walks described here are designed to be paced as slow, very slow, and time to stop, stare, and take photographs.

This is just a small sample of the numerous opportunities for drives and strolls that Lancashire has to offer, and, as the environment

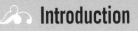

Hollingworth Lake

improves and the tourist potential accelerates, more and more routes are being opened up. I have enjoyed each and every one of the routes described and I hope that my selection will encourage those who read this book to try them all, perhaps revisiting them during each of the four seasons in order to experience Lancashire's glorious scenery in all its rich variety of mood, colour, and texture.

So, lace up your boots, sharpen your appetite, and enjoy a stroll, accompanied by a good brew and a butty.

Ron Freethy

1 Slaidburn

St Andrew's church, Slaidburn

The Walk 5½ miles 2½ hours
Map: OS Landranger 103 Blackburn and Burnley (GR 711525)

How to get there

From the A65 from Long Preston, follow the B6478 and cross the river Ribble. Pass through Wigglesworth and Tosside and pass Stocks reservoir on the right. From Clitheroe, pass through Grindleton and along a minor road signed Slaidburn, passing the hamlet of Harrop Fold on the left. **Parking**: After crossing the Hodder at Slaidburn, there is parking by the river with teashops close by. Alternatively, however, if patronising the Hark to Bounty pub, there is good parking available at the rear.

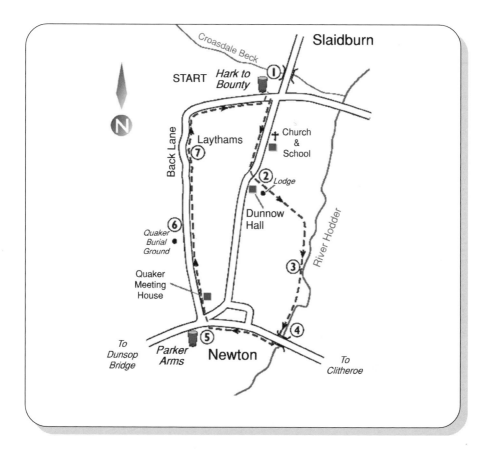

Introduction

Slaidburn is a village dating back to Saxon times. Experts think that the name denotes a sheep pasture close to a stream, although it has been suggested that it marks a long lost battle stone in memory of those killed by the invading Danes in the 9th century. I prefer the sheep option because around the village are terraced fields, called lynchets, which are certainly Saxon and are seen at their best during the winter when frost outlines the slopes of the terraces.

The parish church of St Andrew also serves the village of Newton, and the route retraces that once taken by the inhabitants of Newton on their way to St Andrew's church. They must have found the going tough in bad weather but modern-day strollers are sure of a mix of history, natural history, and gloriously beautiful countryside.

Drive and Stroll

The Hark to Bounty

This is an inn dating back to the 13th century; the building also contains a room which once functioned as a courtroom. Until 1875 it was known as the Dog, but legend has it that a local squire was dining at the inn following a hunting trip. He heard his favourite hound barking and said: 'Hark to Bounty!' and the name stuck.

The hostelry offers bed and breakfast as well as a substantial menu, and visitors are allowed upstairs to see the old courtroom, which operated until 1937. Here are the old benches, and original furnishings. It gives a whole new meaning to the term *called to the bar*. Telephone: 01200 446246.

THE WALK

①

From the **Hark to Bounty**, with its set of stone steps which once led up to the courthouse, turn right. Pass the Youth Hostel on the left and follow the road to **St Andrew's church**. Look to the left, and under certain weather conditions you may see signs of the Saxon lynchets. Next to the church is **Brennand's endowed school**, built in 1717 and still in use.

St Andrew's church has Saxon origins. During Norman and medieval times it served two functions: as a fortress and as a place of worship. The original tower was built as early as the 12th century and its thick walls proved to be of value when the Scots invaded the area in the early 14th century. Still in place is the huge wooden bar, called the 'invasion beam', which secures a solid oak door. Inside, the most unusual artefacts are a couple of 18th century dog whips, which were used to remove unruly animals. It was a custom for worshippers to take the dogs to church with them if they had a long walk and were fearful of being robbed.

Near the school is the Slaidburn Heritage Centre. This is open throughout the year, but from Thursday to Sunday only between October and March. Entry is free (donations welcome) and there is a splendid little teashop run by volunteers. Telephone: 01282 661701.

②

Continue along the **Newton** road and turn left along a footpath to **Dunnow Lodge** and to the left of this is the **River Hodder**. To the right is **Dunnow Hall**, dating mainly from the 18th century, which has a sad tale to tell. It was built by a young man as a future home for his betrothed but the girl died before she could enjoy the glories of the house and its riverside setting.

Hark to Bounty public house

 ③

Follow the obvious footpath, which is a naturalist's delight with the possibility of spotting kingfishers, herons and dippers throughout the year. In summer wildflowers provide colour and scent, whilst in winter the river is the haunt of wildfowl, especially goldeneye and goosander.

(After heavy rain or snow part of this route can be very wet and the appropriate footwear is essential.)

 ④

Approach **Newton Bridge** and turn right into the village. The main hostelry in the village is the **Parker Arms**, which has an extensive car park and also has a varied menu.

 ⑤

From the **Parker Arms**, turn left into **Newton** and take the right fork (*not* the Dunsop Bridge road) and look out for the **Quaker Meeting House** on the right.

The settlement was isolated enough for Quakers, who had been persecuted for their beliefs, to feel safe and a Friends' Meeting House was established in 1767. The Quakers also had a schoolroom, where a young man named John Bright learned his lessons well. He became a fierce social reformer and played a major role in getting the Reform Acts passed in the 1830s. These Acts resulted in many more people being able to vote, a right which we all now enjoy. Near the old Meeting House and situated on the left is the Quakers' burial ground, an area sought out by many Americans in search of their ancestors who fled Britain in order to be able to worship freely in the New World.

Ignore a sign to Dunsop Bridge and follow a metalled track on the right. This narrow attractive road leads back to **Slaidburn** and reveals the **Laythams** area on the right, and **Croasdale Beck**, a tributary of the **Hodder**, can be seen on the left.

This area is the haunt of a few hares and a lot of rabbits. For many years villagers earned a living from rabbits. The meat formed a minor part of their income, but the pelts were of particular importance; they were made into hats, which were sold at markets throughout the area. These were reached via a network of packhorse routes, which are still in evidence today, and the walk is along three of these ancient tracks.

From **Laythams** continue along **Back Lane** and return to the **Hark to Bounty**.

Here is the source of the **river Hodder**, which is a major tributary of the **Ribble**.

2 | West Bradford

Brungerley bridge and the River Ribble

The Walk: 3 miles ⓣAllow 2 hours
Map: OS Landranger 103 Blackburn & Burnley (GR 745445)

How to get there

Turn off the A59 Clitheroe bypass, signed Chatburn. Continue straight on at a roundabout. Pass Castle Cement works on the right. Cross a narrow bridge over the River Ribble and continue into West Bradford village. At the crossroads, turn left to the Three Millstones. Alternatively, there is a bus service to the village from Clitheroe. **Parking**: At the Three Millstones; or on street in the village.

Drive and Stroll

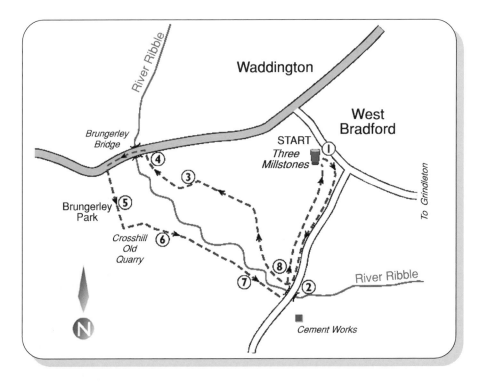

Introduction

This delightful stroll leads not only through glorious countryside but also past the location of one of the most important events to take place during the Wars of the Roses. There is also a nature reserve to explore, offering a variety of wildlife that includes orchids, an abundance of butterflies, and jackdaws and kestrels which avail themselves of the breeding niches provided by the old quarry face.

The Three Millstones

This pub at West Bradford is a welcoming establishment, which was obviously once a substantial farm. From the outside it is easy to identify the old barn, stables, milking parlour, and of course the farmhouse. The name Three Millstones suggests that generations of farmers visited the old watermill (now long gone) to grind their grain into flour. In the past farmers understood the concept of diversification; they sold farm produce and brewed their own ale. The menu today includes some local produce, gammon being a favourite choice. Telephone: 01200 423340.

THE WALK

①

From the **Three Millstones** car park, turn right, and then right again along the road signed to **Clitheroe**. Look for the little stream which runs parallel to the street, and for little bridges which provide access to attractive cottages to the left.

 ②

Approach **West Bradford Bridge** and look for a footpath signed right to **Brungerley**. The route is well signed and initially follows the river. Bear right and cross obvious stiles over lush fields and through a small area of attractive woodland.

 ③

Cross a number of tributary streams leading left down to the **Ribble** and a number of small, long-disused limestone quarries. Pass a farm complex to the right and meet the **Clitheroe to Waddington road** after a slight incline lined with trees.

 ④

Pass through an iron gate and turn left along the road to **Brungerley Bridge.** Take care crossing the narrow bridge, which can be busy with traffic. Just beyond the bridge look out for a sign indicating the **Ribble Way**. Turn left onto a wide track into **Brungerley Park**.

During the Wars of the Roses,

Henry VI, the weak Lancastrian king, was captured by the Yorkists at Brungerley stepping stones over the Ribble. After his defeat at the battle of Hexham in 1464, Henry had sought refuge at several locations in the Ribble Valley and after his capture was sent to London, where he died 'in unusual circumstances'. I think this is historical jargon for 'murdered'.

Later a bridge was built at Brungerley but the stepping – or hipping – stones can still be seen during dry periods. Until 1974 this bridge over the Ribble was the border between Lancashire and Yorkshire, but the whole area is now part of the Red Rose County.

 ⑤

Brungerley Park follows the **Ribble**.

In the early 1900s Brungerley became a place of entertainment when Eli Tucker dammed the Ribble to produce a boating lake and offered 'substantial refreshments'. There are no refreshments these days, but in March botanists visit Brungerley to see the very rare white butterbur growing along the river bank. Also to be found is the more common pink butterbur, the huge leaves of which appear after the flowers and are a feature throughout the summer. Before the invention of greaseproof paper, farmers wrapped up their butter and cheese in the leaves – hence the name butterbur.

Drive and Stroll

Brungerley Park has been laid out alongside disused quarries which have been landscaped. As well as attractive flowers, there are a number of tree sculptures in the park. During the Second World War, the Royal Engineers had a training establishment at Brungerley where troops learned how to construct bridges, as evidenced by the concrete supports that can still be seen.

Continue along the riverside track to **Crosshill Quarry**, which is now a nature reserve managed by the Lancashire Trust for Nature Conservation and partly funded by Castle Cement Limited. Take time to explore the nature reserve and then descend a steep but obvious track leading to a stile.

Cross the stile and follow the riverside path. This has the river on the left and fields on the right. Ignore all stiles to the right but continue along the riverside path, which leads to **West Bradford Bridge**.

A wood sculpture in Brungerley Park

At **West Bradford Bridge** turn left and follow the road to **West Bradford** village and the **Three Millstones**.
(*At this point the Ribble Way footpath continues onwards towards the source of the river via Gisburn, Settle and Ribblehead.*)

3 Waddington

The Parker almshouses

The Walk 2 miles ⏱Allow 1½ hours
Map: OS Landranger 103 Blackburn & Burnley (GR 731438)

How to get there

From Clitheroe follow the B4678 to Waddington. There is a bus service from the Clitheroe Interchange to the village and a rail link from Manchester to Clitheroe via Blackburn. Although it adds a couple of miles to the journey it is pleasant stroll from Clitheroe station to Waddington via Brungerley Bridge and Waddow. **Parking**: At the rear of the Higher Buck Inn, and there is street parking in the village.

Drive and Stroll

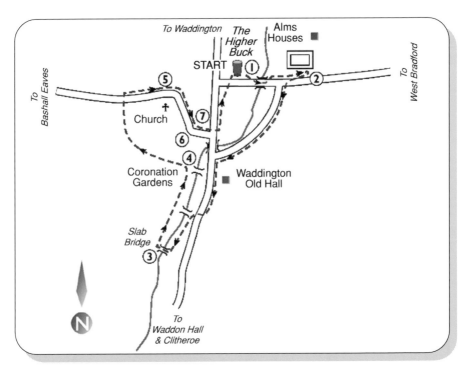

Introduction

Although this is a short stroll, it should not be rushed. A short detour takes in a row of picturesque almshouses and then resumes its streamside course offering a view of historical Waddington Hall and, later, a chance to visit the church of St Helen.

The area was settled by an Anglo-Saxon chief called Wade or Wadda. The Anglo-Saxon Chronicle states that Wadda was implicated in the murder in 794 of Æthelred, who was king of Northumbria. But four years later Wadda got his come-uppance when he was killed in battle at Billington near Whalley.

The Higher Buck

This pub once functioned as a courtroom at the time when this area was used as a hunting forest. The Lower Buck, beyond the church, is further proof that deer (probably the native roe) were once common, and they can still be seen hereabouts. The menu at the Higher Buck has long been famous and includes much local produce, which is well worth sampling. Low beams and warming fires help to create a quiet, cosy atmosphere. Telephone: 01200 423286.

THE WALK

①

From the **Higher Buck** pub turn left and follow the road towards **West Bradford**. Find the almshouses on the left.

The almshouses are set around a spacious green with an old pump in the centre and a lovely little chapel at the rear. This architectural gem can easily be seen from the road, although the privacy of those who live there should be respected.

The Parker Almshouses were once known as Waddington Hospital and were rebuilt by the founder, Robert Parker of Marley Hall in Yorkshire. The entrance gate bears an inscription dating to 1706. Until the boundary changes of 1974, Waddington was in Yorkshire and many of the locals still retain their 'Tyke' connection. The village is divided by a delightful stream, where there are resident grey wagtails and dippers.

② ²

Retrace your steps and turn left into a road running more or less parallel with a small stream to the right.

Continue to follow the stream to the right. Pass a teashop and **Waddington Hall** on the left, and the **Coronation Gardens** on the right.

There are good views of Waddington Hall from the road; however, the property is in private hands and the residents' privacy should be respected. Much of the medieval building would be recognised by Henry VI. He took refuge there during the Wars of the Roses, following his defeat at the battle of Hexham in 1464. Even at this time, parts of the hall were already old and they may date back to the 13th century.

③ ²

After crossing the road to the right, find a small bridge over the stream. Cross this and turn right; to the left are some attractive cottages. Just before **Coronation Gardens** find a set of stone steps. Before climbing them, enjoy a quiet stroll around the gardens, which were laid out in 1953 and are kept in splendid order.

Among attractive seats are plaques indicating that Waddington has won many best kept village awards over the years. There are some Yorkshire plaques dating back to before 1974 when the boundary was changed and then come several awards given by the Lancashire judges. From the gardens there are good views over the stream and road to Waddington Hall.

④ ²

Return to the stone steps to come to two stiles: one leads to the

Drive and Stroll

church, but take the one leading left over the fields. At the road to **Bashall Eaves**, turn right and pass the **Lower Buck** hostelry.

 ⑤

Continue until the church is reached on the right.

The foundation of St Helen is of ancient origin, but the present building dates mainly to 1901, although the architect retained the tower dating to 1501 and kept faithfully to the medieval layout. The church is usually kept open.

When most people could not read or write, church windows were used as a sort of visual aid. The history of Waddington is depicted in the west window, which tells the story of Wadda, of Henry VI, and of course of Helen, the patron saint of the church. She was the mother of Constantine, who was the first Roman emperor to embrace Christianity. Helen was a British princess, and her son was born in York in 274.

 ⑥

From the church, turn right. On the right are the ancient stocks. These show that not all past residents of **Waddington** led blameless lives, but the village today is one of the most idyllic in the county.

 ⑦

From here join the road through the village, turning left and then right to return to the **Higher Buck**.

4 Around Whalley from the Gamecock

Whalley viaduct and the River Calder

The Walk 5 miles ⏱3 hours minimum
Map: OS Landranger 103 Blackburn and Burnley (GR 745340)

How to get there

Whalley itself is situated about 5 miles north-east of Blackburn, between the A59 and the A671. It can also be reached from Burnley via Simonstone and Read. The Gamecock is situated about 1 mile along the A680 towards Clayton-le-Moors. **Parking**: At the Gamecock and along the circular route there is also free parking at Spring Wood and pay and display parking in the centre of Whalley.

Drive and Stroll

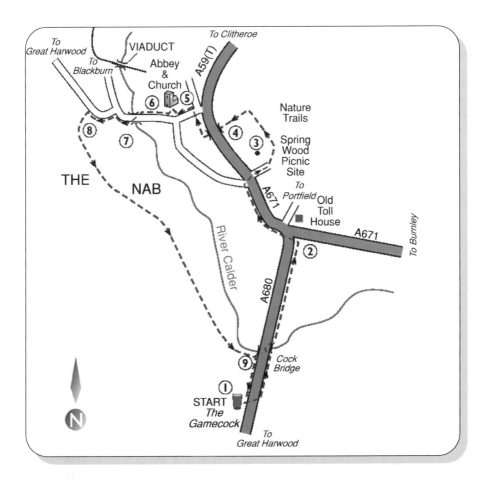

Introduction

Here is spectacular riverside scenery, rich in natural history and ancient history.

The route followed here would have been known to the Cistercian monks who built the abbey, and, long before them, the followers of St Paulinus in the 7th and 8th centuries knew Whalley. In Old English the name means 'the place of the wells'.

The Gamecock Inn

This inn aims to provide family food and fun (there is a children's playground adjacent to the car park). The food is varied, substantial, and tasty.

The exterior and interior show that the building was once a farm. Later, during the 18th and early 19th centuries until the coming of the railway, it was an important inn on the old turnpike road.

There are quiet places, especially in and near the converted milking parlour. Here the stalls (called *boskins*) are still in place, making intimate booths, ideal for having a coffee or a meal whilst planning your walk or discussing the sightings enjoyed at the conclusion of this fascinating stroll. Telephone: 01254 883719.

THE WALK

①

From the **Gamecock** head towards **Cock Bridge**, following the A680 towards **Portfield**.

Cock Bridge spans the A680 over the Calder, and the views down to the river are spectacular. In the summer this is the place to see lapwings, curlews, oyster catchers, and common sandpipers, whilst in winter there are goosanders, goldeneyes and other wildfowl.

At the traffic lights at **Portfield**, look out for the old toll house at the junction and then bear left, now following the A671 towards **Whalley**.

Up to the right is Portfield, which was the site of a Roman signal station. This area has been settled since at least the Iron Age.

Down to the left, where flowers such as wood anemone, primrose, wild garlic and bluebell now thrive, there was once a splendid manor house set on the banks of the Calder. Moreton Hall was built in 1829 on the site of an earlier mansion. It had 365 windows and 52 chimneys, but was demolished in the 1960s.

At the **Whalley** traffic lights turn right into **Spring Wood**, named for the springs which flow through the steep woodland and trickle down into the **Calder**.

At the information centre a free leaflet explains the circular pathway which leads through the woodlands. There are picnic tables overlooking bird-feeding stations. There is also a toilet block, and on most days of the year a small mobile snack bar can be found at the entrance.

Bear left along a wide grassy track and turn left. Look towards the A671 road as it approaches the A59.

Pass over a stile and under a concrete bridge below the A671. (This area can be quite wet, and strong shoes or Wellingtons are essential, especially after rain.) The footpath descent into **Whalley** passes old cottages and farms on both sides. The route twists and turns and crosses a stream via substantial bridges.

23

Drive and Stroll

The River Calder from Whalley Bridge.

The main route into **Whalley** is reached at a junction dominated by the old grammar school. The present building dates to 1725 and is in a splendid state of repair. Turn left at the school, and on the right is the church and abbey. Take time to explore the abbey grounds, which are open daily for a small fee. There is a book shop and a small museum.

The mainly Georgian village is full of shops and neat little cafés, many dating to the early 19th century, when Whalley was at the hub of the turnpike road system. The Whalley Arms, the Dog Inn, and the De Lacy Arms all serve excellent food and drink, and there is also an Indian restaurant.

The road system was later augmented by the railway, and *modern Whalley is overlooked by a wonder of Victorian engineering. This is the 49-arched brick-built viaduct, which was constructed in 1852 and is still functional. It crosses the Calder close to its confluence with the river Ribble.*

Although the abbey was dissolved on the orders of Henry VIII in the late 1530s, large structures do remain. There are regular guided tours, and the well-maintained gardens are a joy. Telephone: 01254 828400.

The parish church of St Mary and All Saints dates to around 1200, but there is evidence of a much earlier religious foundation. In the churchyard there are three ancient crosses. These date from the 9th to the early 11th centuries and are described as Celtic-Scandinavian.

The church is a delight; its interior particularly attracts the historian. Some of the furniture was taken from the old abbey, including the choir stalls with misericords, ledges which allowed the brethren to lean against them whilst standing for the long services. A close look at the carvings reveals that medieval craftsmen had a real sense of humour. There is one showing a man throwing away his sword and kneeling in subjugation to a woman. She is practising the principles of home rule by beating him on the head with a frying pan!

From the church and abbey return to the main road and turn right for 400 yards to reach the bridge. (**Whalley bridge** is an ideal place to stop and stare at the **Calder** and view the railway viaduct.)

From the bridge walk slightly uphill for a short distance before turning left on the old track to **Great Harwood**.

Turn left again onto a signed footpath to **Whalley Nab**. This well-marked but steep track can be wet at times and the appropriate footwear should be worn. **Whalley** is a busy little spot but as soon as the **Nab** (an Old English word meaning 'hill') footpath is reached bird song replaces the hum of traffic.

About $\frac{1}{2}$ mile along the clearly defined footpath is an elevated area providing panoramic views of the **Calder** valley.

At **Cock Bridge** a stone stile opens onto the main A680. A right turn leads back to the **Gamecock**.

5 | Ribchester

Stydd: almshouses in the grand style

The Walk 5½ miles ⏱2½ hours
Map: OS Landranger 103 Blackburn and Burnley (GR 649356)

How to get there

From the A59, between Clitheroe and Preston, turn at traffic lights onto the B6240, signed Ribchester. Cross the Ribble at the De Tabley Arms and follow signs to Ribchester. Turn right into the pay-and-display car park. **Parking**: At the car park (where there are good toilets) or the White Bull Hotel nearby, which has limited parking around it.

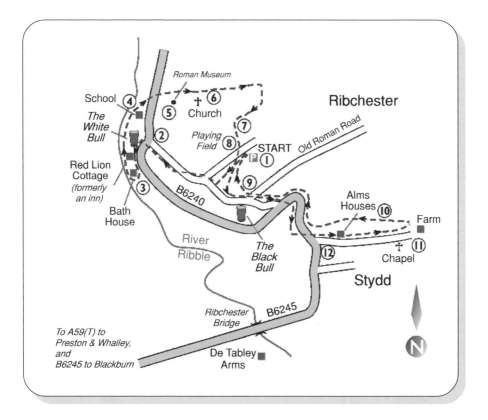

Introduction

Ribchester is the only village situated directly on the banks of the Ribble. In AD 79 the Romans based some 500 cavalry here at a fort named *Brematannacum*. The suffix *Veteranorum* was then added, indicating that retired soldiers were allowed to settle in the area and were given a plot of land. There is thus imperial blood in the veins of some local people no doubt! The route of the walk follows in the footsteps of the Roman legions marching to the fort, which was an important stop on the roads between Chester, Lancaster, Carlisle, and Hadrian's Wall. The stretch by the Ribble (3) can be muddy at times, and so appropriate footwear should be worn.

Most of the cottages in Ribchester date to the 18th century, a time when handloom weaving was in full swing. The lack of a canal or rail link thwarted later efforts to develop the village into a mill town.

Drive and Stroll

To the modern country lover, however, Ribchester is perfect, with riverside views overlooked by sweeping hills. As a consequence, the village provides a large car park and a wide range of gastronomic outlets.

The White Bull

There cannot be many hostelries where customers enter through a porch supported on Roman pillars, but this is the case at the White Bull. An inscription over the door suggests a date of 1707, although this could well have been a rebuild.

Food, including traditional Lancashire dishes, is on offer 'all day every day', and morning tea and coffee are also served. The beamed ceilings add to the charm of one of the county's most historic hostelries. Telephone: 01254 878303.

THE WALK

①

From the car park turn left.

Look for Nora's Tea Rooms, which is based in a cottage dating from 1777 and has a traditional English garden.

To the right is a Roman garden, complete with seats and sculptures added to celebrate the Millennium. The garden itself was laid out with funding from James Openshaw of Hothersall in 1938. A plaque on the ground provides a brief history of the Roman fort.

②

From the garden turn right and follow the weavers' cottages to the **White Bull**, situated on **Water Street**. Turn left along **Water Street** and look out for the **Red Lion** on the right, which is now a pretty cottage, as is the **Old Stables Cottage**, situated opposite; but this once constituted an important coaching inn. Close to the cottage turn right and within a few yards turn right again.

 ③

Pass through a wicket gate. Approach the restored **Roman bath house**, which is run by English Heritage and is open free of charge. A display map identifies the various rooms within the bath house complex. There is a hypocaust (heating system), plus hot and cold rooms.

Bear left and look for a set of steps. Descend these and pass through a wicket gate down to more steps. Turn right and follow the footpath towards the river. Ignore a wicket gate on the left and keep to the path to the right. Follow the path to seats offering views of the **Ribble** to the left. This section of the walk is on the **Ribble Way** long distance footpath.

To the right, behind a stone wall, is

Remains of the Roman bath house, Ribchester

St Wilfrid's Church of England Primary School and at this point the Environment Agency has a river level monitoring station, which indicates that at times of flood the Ribble can be a real danger.

 ④

From the school approach the road through the village and bear left. On the right is the rectory and next right is the **Roman museum**. Straight ahead is the **Ribble Way**, and it is worth following this for about $\frac{1}{2}$ mile and then returning to the museum. The scenery here is magnificent and the wildlife often spectacular.

The museum, which tells the history of the Roman fort, was built in 1914 and has been extended

recently. It is open throughout the year, from Monday to Friday, 9 am to 5 pm, and on Saturday and Sunday from 12 noon to 5 pm. Telephone: 01254 878261.

⑤

Pass through metal gates leading to the parish **church of St Wilfrid**.

In the churchyard are well maintained wooden seats and a sundial set on stone steps to the left. The fine church clock bears the date 1813. The church, which is always open during the day, incorporates many Roman stones, including a pagan altar built into the Norman structure.

⑥

Follow the churchyard track to a

metal gate and turn right onto an obvious footpath but look left to see the ditches and ramparts of the Roman fort, which was oblong in shape. Beyond the ditches are farms and fields leading down to the **Ribble**. Follow the footpath and pass through a wooden kissing gate.

✍ ⑦

Turn sharp right along a paved path. This passes well-maintained tennis courts and a children's playground. Picnic tables have been carefully placed and are well used. This is the site of the Roman parade ground and its shape has altered little over almost 2,000 years. Look for a sandpit to the left and to the right of this a set of stone steps leading back to the car park. Some may prefer to end the walk here but the hamlet of **Stydd** is worth a visit.

✍ ⑧

Return to **Nora's Tearooms** and turn left. At the **Black Bull Inn**, turn right along the B6240, passing the **Ribchester Arms** on the left; then look out for **Stydd Lane** and there

turn left and follow a narrow cul-de-sac to the almshouses.

These date to 1726 and were all built using masonry from the old fort, including a balustrade and a set of pillars. The houses are still in use, and the old well is present but no longer functional.
Continue up the track leading to a farm and to **Stydd** chapel.

This is mainly 12th century but has a fine 13th century doorway built by the Knights Hospitaliers of St John of Jerusalem. The church is open but not used very often. It is the only remaining example of a medieval infirmary chapel. A careful look at the plants growing in the surrounding grounds reveals what may have been a herb garden planted by the knights.

 ✍ ⑨

Retrace your steps to return to the B6240. Turn right here and return to the car park.

6 | Sunnyhurst Wood

Woodland scene at Sunnyhurst

The Walk 5 miles ⏱3 hours
Map: OS Explorer 19 West Pennine Moors or OS Landranger 103 Blackburn & Burnley (GR 681226)

How to get there

Sunnyhurst is well signed from the A666 Blackburn to Darwen Road, which can be reached from junction 4 of the M65. Keep following the brown signs along Earnsdale Road, Sunnyhurst Lane and Tockholes Road. **Parking**: There is a small car park situated between the Lych Gate restaurant (left) and Sunnyhurst pub (right).

Drive and Stroll

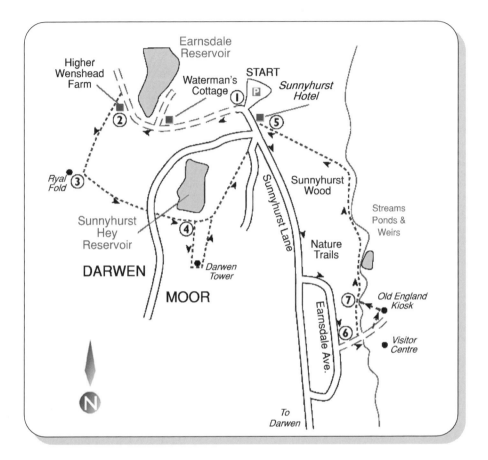

Introduction

Dominating this walk, which includes a few places where the going is steep and tough, is the 86ft high Jubilee Tower, which stands 1225ft above sea level on Darwen Moor and is open free of charge. The Sunnyhurst area was planted up in the early 19th century to provide cover for game birds. In 1902 it was purchased by public subscription and is freely open as a woodland park. There are now around seven miles of footpaths meandering over 85 acres. Those with time to spare should extend this walk by following some of these paths. Entrance is free. Leaflets are available from the visitor centre sited in the old gamekeeper's cottage, which is open on Tuesdays, Thursdays, Saturdays and Sundays between 2 pm and 4.30 pm (01254 701545).

The Old England Kiosk

In the woodland on the banks of Earnsdale Brook is the Old England Kiosk. It was built in 1912 to commemorate the coronation of George V and serves a wide selection of drinks, snacks and meals. The gentle atmosphere of yesteryear is maintained, and, since it is licensed to hold civil marriages, it is not surprising that some couples are now celebrating their wedding here in period style. Telephone: 01254 701503.

THE WALK

①

From the car park, turn right along a track leading to **Waterman's Cottage**, which was built in 1897. Beware of a confusing directional sign and be sure to bear left and ascend the track.

Earnsdale Reservoir is visible down to the right. This was built in 1854 to provide essential water as the cotton industry around Darwen expanded very quickly. On the hills beyond is Darwen Golf Club.

Approach **Higher Wenshead Farm** and continue straight ahead, keeping the farm on the left. Pass through a stone gate, continue ahead, and cross a stile at the next farm gate. Where the farm track bears right, take the first of two stiles.

✍ ②

Bear left and climb the steps up the moorland towards **Darwen Tower**, which is signed.

At the top of the steps turn right and look for **Owd Aggie's**, which is now just a ruined cottage. The name refers to a former owner who in 1860 was murdered by thieves.

Legend (unconfirmed but romantic) tells us that the area here was called Stepback because Cromwell was marching his troops and during a storm he said 'Step back; we will go no further'. This sounds like legend to me, as Cromwell was not known to have taken a step backwards! The red grouse, which is still found on the moor, has a call which sounds like 'Step back'; I prefer this explanation!

✍ ③

Turn left near a bench which overlooks **Stepback Clough**. Pass over a stile and turn left where there is a stone waymark. Here are fine views to the left, and at **Ryal Fold** to the right there is a group of farms and attractive cottages, a car park, and a pub.

Continue along the track, looking out for **Sunnyhurst Hey Reservoir** on the left.

This came on stream in 1875 as Darwen demanded more and more water to help crown King Cotton. There is a stone above the path which carries a benchmark

Waterman's Cottage

indicating an elevation of 1,220 feet.

↪ ④

Darwen Tower is signed along a short path to the right. This is open daily and the top is reached by a flight of stone steps.

The tower was completed in 1897 at a cost of £650 to celebrate the diamond jubilee of Queen Victoria. It also provided a celebration for local walkers, who had just won a court case against the owner of the grouse moor, allowing them to wander freely over the moor.

The view from the top is spectacular and includes the Cumbrian mountains, the Isle of Man, the Ribble Valley, and much of the area covered by the strolls in this book.

Look out for an Ordnance Survey trig point and here turn right to rejoin the track. At the next junction carry straight on, the track then sweeps to the right. The alternative route leads down into **Darwen** town centre. Follow the path downhill, with a wall and banking on the left. Do not pass through the kissing gate but keep this on your right. Look left as the path descends close to the water treatment works associated with **Sunnyhurst Hey Reservoir.**

⑤

Pass through a metal kissing gate and where the path forks bear left. This descends to the **Sunnyhurst Hotel**.

A left turn leads back to the car park (for those who are tired), but the present walk continues into **Sunnyhurst Wood**. Turn right at the pub and then immediately left onto **Sunnyhurst Lane**. Descend and then turn left along **Earnsdale Avenue** and then **Earnsdale Road**. Ignore a lych gate shelter on the left and the path down into the woods.

⑥

Continue along **Earnsdale Road**, looking out for an information board; turn left here and descend a steep track down from the information centre and the Old England Kiosk and café. A sign nearby indicates a circular nature trail dedicated to Herbert Parkinson. This adds another 2 miles to the route, but is well worth it.

⑦

On returning to the Kiosk keep the stream on the right and pass artificial waterfalls, quaint bridges, and a small lake, which is an ideal place to watch winter waterfowl.

Following a flood in 2002 some paths have had to be diverted. Pass a gazebo on the right and then bear left following a steep path. This leads up to the lych gate, after which a right turn leads back to the car park.

7 | Hurst Green

Cromwell's Bridge

The Walk 6 miles ⊕ 3 hours
Maps: OS Landranger 103, Blackburn and Burnley; OS Explorer 19 West Pennine Moors (GR 689384)

How to get there

From Clitheroe follow the B6243, which links Mitton and Longridge, or on the M6 from Preston follow the signs to Longridge and then join the B6243 to Hurst Green. **Parking**: There is safe village parking in Hurst Green, close to the Shireburn Arms; on the opposite side of the road is a toilet block. There is also roadside parking close to Stonyhurst School.

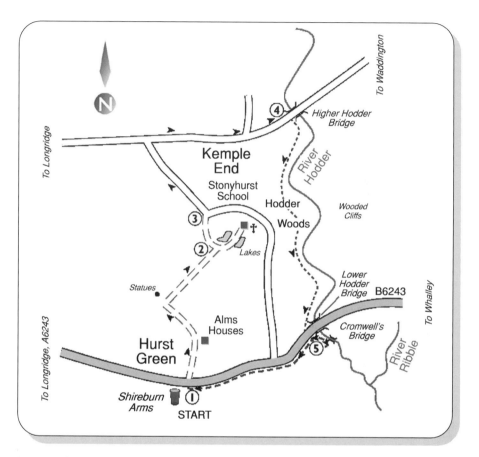

Introduction

This walk encompasses lovely woods and glorious buildings. Stonyhurst College, lying on the northerly edge of Hurst Green, is a celebrated Catholic boarding school, whose distinguished old boys include Sir Arthur Conan Doyle (it is said that many of the scenes and locations in *The Hound of the Baskervilles* were based on Hurst Green and the surrounding moors) and the actor Charles Laughton. More recent literary associations include Gerard Manley Hopkins, who was a teacher there, and J.R.R. Tolkien, two of whose sons were educated at the school.

The route follows the bank of the Hodder, the water of which is often stained brown with peat. In *Lord of the Rings* the river is called the Brandywine. There is now a flourishing Tolkien Trail, which allows enthusiasts to follow the hobbits and seems set to become a major tourist attraction.

Drive and Stroll

The Bayley Arms and the Shireburn Arms

These two pubs are both pleasant places to eat. The Shireburn offers a variety of local produce as well as what can be described as a traditional menu. Tea and coffee are served throughout the day.

There are lots of quiet corners in which to enjoy the food on offer and read a chapter of *The Hobbit*, *Lord of the Rings*, or perhaps *Hound of the Baskervilles*. Accommodation is available for those who want to spend more time in the area. Telephone: 01254 826518.

At times when the pupils of the school are on holiday light snacks are available at the school.

THE WALK

①

From the **Shireburn**, cross the B6243 and follow a gentle incline up into the village. Pass the **Bayley Arms** on the right, a line of attractive cottages on the left and then a splendid group of almshouses on the right. At one time these were situated on the nearby hillside at **Kemple End**. By 1947 they were all but derelict, but they were then moved stone by stone and rebuilt in the heart of the village and used as accommodation for school workers.

Continue along the narrow road through a woodland area. Find a religious statue on the left and then look right; the view across to the school is magnificent.

Follow the long drive up to the school. The buildings overlook a couple of large lakes, which are the haunt of introduced and native waterfowl. The road turns sharp left in front of the school gates.

The Sherburn (or Shireburn) family were staunch Catholics and survived all the religious upheavals only for the male line to fail. The infant son of Sir Nicholas died in 1702 from eating yew berries. Nicholas himself died in 1717, and the property passed to his daughter, who had married the Duke of Norfolk. After her death the Weld family inherited, and in 1794 they leased the mansion to the Jesuits, who founded the school, which has thrived ever since.

The school is pleased to welcome visitors during the holidays. The gardens are open from July 1 to August 25, from Saturday to Thursday (1–5 pm); the college and its magnificent library are open from July 14 to August 25, from Saturday to Thursday (1–4 pm). Telephone: 01254 826345.

②

Follow the winding road, keeping the school on the right. (You may think that you are walking on too

Stonyhurst College

much tarmac but this is just the place to do it. It was on these roads in 1826 that John L. MacAdam first tried out his now famous construction methods.)

 ③

At the junction between the school track and a minor road turn left. Continue for $\frac{1}{2}$ mile and turn right at a crossroads. On the right is a little car park at **Kemple End**. Look out for the foundations of the old almshouses.

④

The road descends to another T-junction; here turn right and descend to the **Higher Hodder Bridge**. Look up at a complex of apartments which were once the popular **Higher Hodder Inn**. Before the bridge find a footpath indicated through a wall and turn right, in the direction of **Lower Hodder Bridge**.

Next comes almost 1 mile of magnificent woodland with the **River Hodder** on the left. Botanists flock to this area in spring, and there is yet another literary connection: the Jesuit poet Gerard Manley Hopkins (1844–89) composed *The Hodder Woods* as he strolled this route. He was a master at the school.

⑤

Approach **Lower Hodder Bridge** and cross the road. Look from the bridge to see one of the most famous packhorse bridges in Britain. This was built in 1562. It has recently been restored and has won many awards. Locally it is called **Cromwell's Bridge**, and it is said that in August 1648 Cromwell's troops crossed it. The span is too narrow to allow ordnance to pass and so they also used the ford, which can still be seen below.

From **Cromwell's Bridge** turn left onto the road and follow it back to **Hurst Green**. The scenery on both sides of the road is as fine as anywhere in Lancashire.

8 | Witton Park and Hoghton Tower

The rose window at Pleasington Priory

The Walk 6 miles ⏱3 hours
Map: Explorer 19 West Pennine Moors or Landranger 103 Blackburn & Burnley (GR 658275).

How to get there

Witton Park is almost in the centre of Blackburn and reached off the A674 along Preston Old Road. **Parking**: There is a large car park at the entrance to the park, and a toilet block. From this area a narrow road leads up to the visitor centre, where there is some parking but this is limited, especially during busier periods.

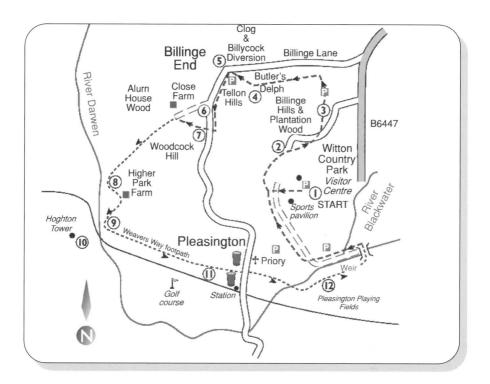

Introduction

This walk follows part of the Witton Weavers' Way. Information leaflets describe this track as an up hill and down dale route, but for almost all the way the going is easy. It passes close to the River Darwen and by the side of a nature reserve, and provides an opportunity to explore Pleasington Priory. There are reminders of two historic houses, at Witton itself and Hoghton Tower.

The riverside scenery typical of this walk is improving thanks to massive clean-ups coordinated by the water company, the Environment Agency, and the Darwen River Valley Initiative. Farmland and riparian habitats combine to provide idyllic scenery in an area close to the urban sprawls of Preston, Chorley and Blackburn.

Witton Country Park

Witton Country Park was once the power base of the Feilden family. Their early manor house was replaced in 1800 and surrounded by an estate of 480 acres (195 hectares). In 1946 Blackburn Corporation bought the

Drive and Stroll

estate but in 1954 demolished the main house, which by then was almost falling down.

The coach houses, outhouses and stables were retained and the estate developed into a country park and playing fields complex. Part of the stables is now a delightful little café and tearoom (for details of opening ring 01254 53277).

The café prides itself on an excellent brew of tea and a selection of snacks, sandwiches and cakes.

For those walking in the evening when the café is closed, this walk passes several hostelries including the Clog and Billycock (telephone: 01254 207151), the Butler's Arms, the Railway, and – by adding about a mile to your journey – the historic Sirloin in Hoghton village.

THE WALK

①

Start from the **Witton Park Visitor Centre** and take time to look at the domestic animals and the small mammal centre. Opposite the café is the carriage house, which has displays of old vehicles and farm machinery. (Details on opening times, etc, and leaflets can be obtained from the Tourist Information Centre; telephone: 01254 681120.) Stroll to the sports pavilion.

 ②

From the right of the sports pavilion turn right along the road towards a belt of trees. At the edge of this building turn right along a fence, cross a footbridge, and follow the obvious track through a wood.

Pass through a kissing gate and cross fields to **Higher Gardens Plantation**, which is on the right. Climb a stile and ascend a path through the woods to **Kilnyard Lane**.

There is a car park here and an ideal place to picnic, especially on hot days when the park is busy.

 ③

Turn left along **Billinge Lane**, right through a gateway, and then left into **Billinge Wood**. It is thought that the name Billinge is derived from the Old English word 'biling' meaning hill or sharp ridge – there is a Billinge Hill nearby.

 ④

Carry straight on at the next junction and climb a stile on the left corner, where there is another car park. Cross a field and go over a stile to the brow of a hill, where there is a long-disused quarry. Descend the track through the field and keep the fence on the left.

(**Warning:** Behind the fence, in **Butler's Delph Quarry** (*delph* derived from Old English *delfan* 'to dig or mine'), the face of the old workings (once owned by the

Butler family of Pleasington Hall) is very steep, unstable, and dangerous.

At the bottom of the next field, climb a stile. The name of the area sounds like a Western film; **the Yellow Hills**, however, seem to be aptly named for the colour of the gorse which dominates the area.

Turn left along a lane. A short diversion leads to an attractive group of 18th century handloom cottages and the **Clog and Billycock pub**, so named because a landlord of long ago wore clogs and a billycock hat.

There is soon a right turn into another wood.

About 50 yards into the wood take care when following a rather indistinct right fork. Cross a stile and look for a gate and head straight for it. After passing through the gate climb a stile and soon reach a minor road linking **Billinge End** and the village of **Pleasington**. This earns its name and is very pleasant indeed. The name, however, actually means the *tun* ('settlement') associated with a man called Plesa.

Here is the region called **Woodcock Hill** and this species of woodland wading bird is still found in the area. Approach a bend and follow the public footpath signed off to

A wood sculptures in Witton Park

the left towards **Close Farm**.

Behind the farm is yet more woodland and nearby are the remains of a medieval alum mine, which produced huge revenues for the de Hoghtons. Alum is an aluminous shale which until the invention of synthetic dyes during the Industrial Revolution was used as a mordant in dyeing cloth.

Keep straight ahead along a field, follow a hedge on the right and cross another stile to the right of a prominent gully. Continue straight ahead, cross the gully, and bear right. At the end of an open field look to the right for a valley lined with trees. Follow this track to the bank of the **River Darwen**.

At this point bear left and head

Drive and Stroll

towards **Higher Park Farm**. There is a stile at the corner of the farm buildings; climb this, and go past the farmhouse and through a gate.

Turn left and keep the river on your right. Follow the bend of the river to the right, where you will see the imposing bulk of **Hoghton Tower**.

The site on which Hoghton stands has been the family home of the de Hoghtons since the time of William the Conqueror. Hoghton Tower is open to the public but the times vary; to avoid disappointment, it is advisable to check by telephone (01254 852986) or on the web site, which is updated regularly (www.hoghtontower.co.uk).

This route shows off the tower to its best advantage, as it is set on a steep outcrop of rock overlooking the Darwen. Here is the ideal medieval compromise of family home and defensive fortress. Although the tower has been added to and restored over the years, the strength, which was essential during the 15th and 16th centuries, has been retained.

There is firm evidence that young William Shakespeare performed at the tower, and in 1617 the de Hoghtons almost bankrupted themselves by entertaining King James I there.

Continue along the river to a bridge. Turn left along a track to the right of which is **Pleasington Golf Club**. Pass through a stile to the right, and at a second stile cross an open field. Climb out of a valley, then over another stile and follow the track to **Pleasington** village. There are two excellent hostelries in the village: the **Butler's Arms** and the **Railway**.

(The following section of the walk can be enjoyed by those who wish to visit Pleasington by train from either Blackburn or Preston.)

From **Pleasington Lane** cross over and follow a rough but obvious track to **Pleasington Playing Fields**, passing **Pleasington Priory** on the left.

This is not a medieval priory but a Roman Catholic church built in 1819 to celebrate the easing of the persecution of the Old Religion. It was built in the Gothic style and has a wonderful rose window. The doorway is in the style of the Norman period and some masonry was actually brought from the ruins of Whalley Abbey.

Cross the football pitch and then go on to the road. Cross the road bridge over the river and then take the immediate left alongside the **River Darwen**. This leads back to the main car park at **Witton**.

9 Pilling

Cockling on Pilling beach at low tide

The Walk 5 miles ⏱3 hours
Map: OS Landranger 102 Preston & Blackpool (GR 416492)

How to get there

Pilling is reached along the A588 and the village is at the end of a coastal cul-de-sac. **Parking**: There is parking alongside the Golden Ball Hotel and to the left of a road leading from the church, where there is also a clean toilet block, shops, and Old Carr Farm Tea Rooms. There is also good parking on the roadside opposite the sands.

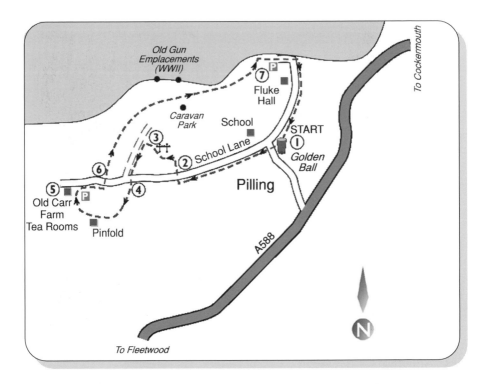

Introduction

Pilling is still a farming village but has also earned a good living from fishing, especially shellfishing. Cockling is particularly important and supplies are delivered to resorts such as Blackpool. Specially designed forks, rakes, and nets make collecting cockles easier.

The Golden Ball

This pub has a varied menu (telephone: 01253 790212), but if you fancy a hearty breakfast, lunch, or a snack then Old Carr Farm Tea Rooms is a delight. It is just what it seems to be, an old farmhouse specialising in home-produced food and preserves, and it offers one of the best cups of tea to be found anywhere.

When I follow this walk, I start with tea and scones with home-made jam, and at the end of the ramble finish off with a breakfast (which is served all day). Local preserves are on sale, and in the yard there are plants for sale and bric-à-brac from the junk shop. Telephone: 01253 790249.

Sundial on the old church

THE WALK

①

From the car park next to the **Golden Ball** follow **School Lane** towards the church. This area is full of flowers almost throughout the year and looks cared for, as befits a village which has won several awards.

 ②

From the lane, turn right along the path to the modern church and follow it round the grounds to a wicket gate, with a caravan site away in the background to the right. Pass through a field, often

with grazing cattle, and through another gate. This leads to the cemetery and the old church. After exploring the church, pass through an avenue of yew trees to a gate.

The village's two churches are both dedicated to St John the Baptist. On the wall of the older church is a sundial memorial to the Revd G. Holden, dated 1766 and inscribed 'Thus Eternity approacheth'; it keeps surprisingly good time. George Holden was fascinated by tidal movements and is credited with inventing the first set of tide tables. Thanks to the efforts of the Churches Conservation Trust, the old church is well maintained. A date of 1717 is recorded over the arch; and on the door is a note indicating where the key can be obtained.

🏳 ③

Turn left and head towards the road through the village.

🏳 ④

Cross the road and look out for a footpath signed 'Pinfold'. Pass through trees and an overgrown footpath to the old village sheepfold.

Stray sheep were once impounded there until owners identified them by examining their ear (or lug) marks. This practice dates back to Saxon times and ceased only in the last century.

Continue along the track, which can be overgrown in the summer because it is not much used. Approach old farm buildings to the right and left. Bear right and pass through a gate.

🏳 ⑤

Turn right and reach a car park and toilet block close to the road

through the village. Here on the left is the **Old Carr Farm** restaurant and teashop.

🏳 ⑥

From **Old Carr Farm** cross the road and look out for a faded sign pointing left. This leads over fields for about 1 mile and reaches Pilling beach, where there is another car park.

Pilling beach is always popular, whatever the state of the tide. At low water the clean sands and mud flats are ideal for collecting cockles. There is excellent bird watching in all seasons. Along the sea defence wall there are remnants of old gun emplacements dating back to the Second World War, when it was thought that a German invasion might come via southern Ireland.

🏳 ⑦

Turn right at the sands and join the narrow road for just over a mile. Pass **Fluke Hall** on the right and take advantage of the seats arranged to face the fields and the sea. Return along **School Lane** to the car park by the **Golden Ball**.

10 Chipping

Chipping Main Street

The Walk 5½miles ⊕2½ hours
Maps: OS Landranger 103 Blackburn & Burnley and 102 Preston & Blackpool (GR 624433)

How to get there

From Preston leave the M6 at Junction 31a and follow the B6243 to Longridge and then follow minor roads to Chipping. From Clitheroe follow the B6245 to Longridge. **Parking**: There is a car park in Church Raike which is reached by turning right straight after Cobbled Corner.

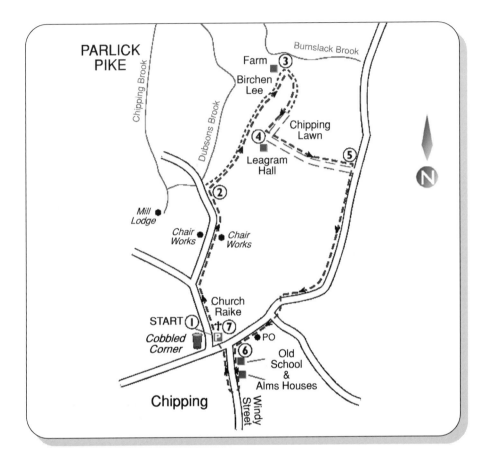

Introduction

This stroll leads through some of the most beautiful countryside in Britain, Leagram Park having remained unspoiled since medieval days, when it was a deer park.

There is a local saying that 'all roads lead to Chipping'. This is not surprising, considering that the word chipping simply means 'market'. In medieval times trading was carried on in the churchyard; people walked miles to worship and it made sense to hold a market after the service. The village is overlooked by the hulk of Parlick Pike, a favourite location for hang gliders.

There are three pubs in the village: the Sun, the Talbot, and the Tillotson's Arms, all dating back to the coaching era of the 19th century. They offer a wide menu, including lots of Lancashire dishes.

Berry's chairworks

The Cobbled Corner

My stop is at the Cobbled Corner (telephone: 01996 61551; www.cobbledcorner.co.uk), which is a family owned restaurant serving snacks and more substantial meals, most of which are fresh and home made. My favourite is the Lancashire hotpot with pickled cabbage. The home-made pies and scones are popular with walkers, cyclists, and the stream of tourists. Children are always welcome, and there is a half-price menu, as well as a very useful take out service for picnickers. There are also themed evenings.

THE WALK

①

From the car park turn left along **Church Raike**. Where the narrow road forks, bear right to descend the steep road.

Berry's chair works is situated in a dip through which **Chipping Brook** runs. Look out for a set of stone steps leading down to the stream once used by the cottagers as a washing up point. The chair works has its own sawmill and the smell of cut wood is one of the joys of this stroll.

Pass the sawmill on the left and ascend the narrow road to the old mill lodge, which is as full of interesting wildlife as a nature reserve. Look down to the left to see the mill leet and the old waterwheel mounting, which has been retained although it has not worked for many years.

⤷ ②

Look carefully to the right about halfway along the lodge path. Almost hidden in the vegetation is a signpost. Turn right and almost immediately look for a stile with a yellow arrow on it. Cross to the right over this stile.

The next 1¾ miles leads towards an area known as **Burnslack**. Initially the track rises steeply and a hedgerow must be followed closely, ignoring a number of farm gates. Look out for panoramic views of **Parlick Pike**.

Take care as parts of this section are not well marked. Follow a hollow area and keep to the incline, heading straight for **Birchen Lee Farm**. Cross a stile and cross a footbridge to **Burnslack**.

⤷ ③

At **Birchen Lee Farm** (a date stone on the house reads J.N. 1867), turn sharp right and follow the now obvious track to **Chipping Lawn**.

⤷ ④

Turn right and follow the clear track through the grounds of **Leagram Hall**, which is visible on the right.

⤷ ⑤

Descend from Leagram down to a narrow road and here turn right

and then right again into **Chipping** village.

Look for the Post Office on the left and examine a wall plaque. This records that John Brabin once lived in the house. He made his fortune from textiles and founded a school and almshouses in 1683.

Continue through the village and find **Windy Street**, turning left here. A few yards along the very narrow street you will find the almshouses and the old school on the left. These are now private residences and are kept in splendid repair. Return along **Windy Street** to the junction with the village street.

⤷ ⑥

Opposite is the church, which is set on a hill and reached by a set of impressive stone steps and a metal gate.

St Bartholomew's is one of the most interesting churches in Lancashire and dominates the village. There was a church on the site from 1041, but the main construction period dates to 1240, and the sturdy tower was built in 1540.

The stained glass is both ancient and modern, with a recent window dedicated to the Berry family who still operate the world famous chair and furniture works.

From the church return to the car park via the **Cobbled Corner Café**.

11 Overton and Sunderland Point

Sunderland Point

The Walk There is a long option of about 6 miles from Overton or a shorter 2-mile circular trail just around Sunderland Point. There are toilets on the foreshore at Sunderland but *no* refreshments. ⓘFor the long walk allow $3\frac{1}{2}$ hours and for the shorter stroll allow $1\frac{1}{2}$ hours.
Map: OS Landranger 97 Kendal & Morecambe (GR 431582)

How to get there

From Lancaster take the A683 signed to Heysham and Morecambe. After $2\frac{1}{2}$ miles follow signs indicating left to Overton. From Morecambe take the coastal road and follow the signs for Overton. **Parking**: There is limited parking at the church of St Helen, reached by turning first left off the main street. There is a free car park opposite the Globe Hotel, which is the last building before the tidal causeway leads out to Sunderland Point.

Drive and Stroll

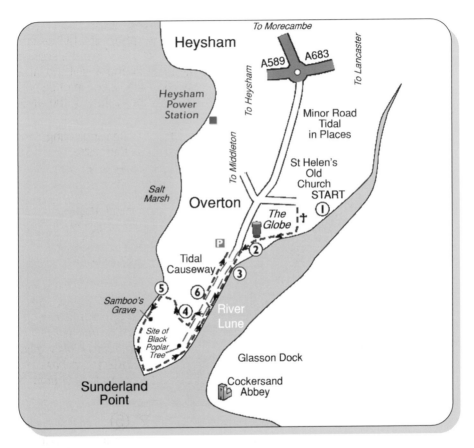

Introduction

I have walked this route for more than 30 years, and each visit has been different.

Throughout the walk there are sweeping panoramic vistas, with good views across the Lune estuary to Glasson Dock and in the distance the splendidly proportioned chapter house – all that is left – of Cockersand Abbey.

This is everything a stroller could ask for, but **do ensure that you are fully aware of tide times**. Danger periods are indicated by prominent signs, but a set of tide tables should be carried; these can be purchased from the local newsagent. You could also ask locals or at the Globe.

The Globe

Built in the 1600s, the Globe at Overton stands at the gateway to Sunderland

Point and became the haunt of sailors working the West Indies route. Many years later, around the turn of the 19th century, the Globe was the central feature of Overton Pleasure Gardens, a photograph of which can be seen in the bar. River Lune salmon dominated the menu then and is still available today when in season as part of a varied and wholesome selection of dishes. Available at the bar is a free leaflet which explains the history of the area. Telephone: 01524 85822.

THE WALK

1. From the church walk towards the village and after a few yards find a footpath signed **'Sunderland Point Causeway'**. Enjoy the glorious views and after just over a mile turn right along the estuary to the **Globe**.

The parish **church of St Helen** dates back to Saxon times (the west wall is without doubt Saxon), but its most famous feature is the very early Anglo-Norman doorway, which has been dated to around 1050.

②

As the **Globe** comes into view, turn left onto the causeway to **Sunderland**. Those who only want a short stroll may wish to drive along the causeway (about a mile) and park on the shingle preshore near the toilet block.

Walking the metalled causeway provides views of mud flats which abound with birds at all times but especially in winter.

③

Turn left at the toilet block and halfway through **Sunderland** turn

sharp right at a sign indicating **West Shore** and **Carr Lane**.

The sandy track climbs gently to the **Sunderland Point Mission Church** on the left. Opposite is a house where there is a book on sale explaining the history of **Sunderland Point**.

Sunderland Point, which, second only to Bristol, was once the most important harbour on the west coast, has not functioned as a port since the early 1800s and has been caught in a wonderful time warp.

⑤

Continue along a narrow tree-lined track to a metal gate and here turn left and follow the estuary shore. For some reason this route is not marked, but there is an obvious right of way along the well-worn path.

Look out for a wood and metal seat on the left. Beyond this is a finger post and a set of stone steps leading to **Samboo's grave**. His is surely one of the most beautiful resting paces in the world.

In 1801 no less than 76 ships,

Samboo's grave

each of more than 160 tons, were trading from the port. They were sometimes moored four and five deep across the Lune and laden with sugar, rum, tobacco, mahogany and sadly also slaves.

One of the slaves, named Samboo, died at Sunderland around 1735. It was not allowed to bury him in consecrated ground but in 1786 a stone slab was placed on his seashore resting place. Visitors and residents bring flowers and children even leave toys as a mark of respect.

From the grave continue left along the shoreline to another unlocked metal gate. (Don't forget to close the gate behind you as you enjoy the plant and bird life.) The track is level here but the going becomes difficult because of the mix of pebbles and boulders.

On the other side of the estuary are **Glasson Dock** and the **Cockers and Abbey Chapter House**. The track climbs gently to a colonial style house, obviously dating back to the days of the cotton trade but still in an excellent state of repair.

For more than 200 years the so-called cotton tree grew on the harbour side but on January 1st 1998 a storm blew the tree down. Subsequent studies have shown the tree to have been a black poplar, which is a very rare native to Britain.

From the old cotton tree area return along **Second Terrace** to the toilet block and then right along the causeway, to the **Globe** and the church.

12 | Garstang

Greenhalgh Castle

The Walk 3 miles ⏱2½ hours
Map: OS Landranger 97 Kendal & Morecambe (GR 494455)

How to get there

From the M6 Junction 32 join the A6 and follow signs to Broughton. Go straight on at Broughton traffic lights and then through Bilsborrow. Turn right on the B6430 through Catterall to Garstang. Approach the centre of Garstang and turn left to the Tythe Barn, which is signed. **Parking**: The Tythe Barn has a very large car park. Alternatively, there is a large pay-and-display car park on the riverbank close to the town centre, which is well signed from all directions. It is close to the discovery and information centre (telephone 01995 602125) and there are excellent toilet facilities here. The site is within range of lots of shops, pubs, snack bars and restaurants.

Drive and Stroll

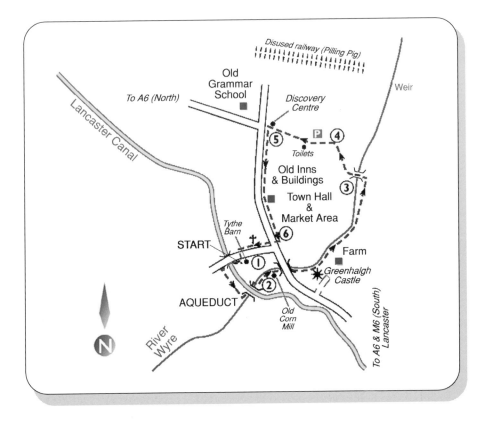

Introduction

This mostly level stroll involves exploring a canal towpath and a riverbank. There are panoramic views over the old market town of Garstang and to the 15th century ruin of Greenhalgh Castle, which is set on a prominent hill.

To the canal historian this stretch of the Lancaster is a fascinating lesson in the design of aqueducts and bridges, whilst the naturalist can enjoy spring birds, summer flowers, autumn fruits and winter wildfowl.

The Tythe Barn

This pub dates at least to the 15th century, and its exposed beams are as sturdy now as on the day it was built. Hung from the beams, set in alcoves, or secured to the walls are artefacts relating to the old crafts of the area, including farm implements and the tools of cobblers, wheelwrights, blacksmiths and coopers. They all look sharp enough for a craftsman to start work as soon as he has finished his lunch or his last pint.

The furniture is also interesting. There is a huge trestle table down the centre of the room and a number of benches set in cosy alcoves. These came from a local chapel. In winter a huge log fire burns and adds to an atmosphere which is all the more welcome to those who have just completed this circular hike through history.

The food on offer at the Tythe Barn is a combination of modern and traditional Lancashire fare. The Lancashire hotpot and pickled cabbage is my favourite. Occasionally medieval feasts are organised. Telephone: 01995 604486.

THE WALK

①

From **Th'owd Tythe Barn** turn left and then cross the road. Turn left again and go over the canal bridge. Cross the bridge road with care and then descend stone steps onto the **Lancaster Canal** towpath. Turn right.

To the left the **Tythe Barn** looks delightful in its setting directly on the basin of the canal. Whatever the season there are always boats here, as British Waterways provide permanent moorings. Waterfowl are always in evidence but on the wall of the hostelry is a dovecote, which attracts domesticated and wild species.

Continue along the canal towpath, soon reaching a splendidly proportioned aqueduct.

The Lancaster Canal was opened in 1797, and because of this cut Garstang increased in prosperity. There was, however, something of a downturn in the 1840s when the

Lancaster to Preston railway opened. The elders of the town were somewhat short-sighted because they thought that the mania for railways would soon disappear and the glory days of canals and coach roads would return. Garstang was therefore by-passed by the railway but part of its attraction now is that it has become trapped in a time warp dating back to the coaches and horses of the early 19th century.

②

At the aqueduct turn right and descend a steep wooden staircase leading down to the banks of the river and an important stopping point on the long distance footpath called the **Wyre Way**. Turn right and pass under the aqueduct, where the skill of the late 18th century masons can be appreciated. A footpath follows the bank of the **Wyre**, which is on the left. By the bank is a series of reed fringed ponds.

Follow the riverside path to the **Old Corn Mill** and pass through the

Drive and Stroll

Overlooking the canal basin to the Tythe Barn

18th century complex, which is now being used as a residential home. (A look to the left reveals the old millrace, though it no longer carries water.) Cross the road at the old mill and rejoin the footpath beside the **Wyre**. Continue until the ruin of **Greenhalgh Castle** is seen surmounting a hill to the right.

Greenhalgh, built on the orders of the Earl of Derby in 1490, was quite late in terms of castles. The earl's object was to control the important crossing of the River Wyre. Only a couple of stout walls now remain, because in 1649 the Royalist garrison resisted Cromwell and was one of the last to surrender *to the Roundheads, who, determined that no Cavaliers would ever return, almost completely demolished the building. Over the years the ruin was used by local people as an unofficial and very inexpensive quarry.*

Although the route does not include the field footpath up to the castle, which is on private land, it is worth the well-marked extra mile there and back. A concessionary stile has been provided to allow access to the castle mound, from which there are views over farms and fields to a bend of the **River Wyre**.

✍ ③

Continue along this path until an

obvious left-hand path leads alongside a sports field to an obvious riverside track. This is well supplied with seats and is a perfect spot to enjoy a picnic in idyllic surroundings.

A look to the right will reveal an old pig, which, however, is not an animal but a long disused railway line. This was not part of the main line but a farmers' link between Garstang, Pilling and Knott End, which is on the estuary of the river Wyre. Locals compared the sound of the locomotives to that of a screaming pig – hence the affectionate name of the Pilling Pig. The line opened in 1908 and closed in 1950.

 ④

Continue along this track, heading left to the extensive pay-and-display car park by the **River Wyre**. Here is situated the discovery and information centre.

On the opposite side of the main thoroughfare through Garstang is the arts centre, which was once the town's grammar school. This was built in 1792 and continued to function until 1928.

 ⑤

Turn left along the main road to **Market Square** and discover the old coaching town with its inns, alleys and shops.

The market is still held on its original site. A charter for a market was granted by Edward II in 1310 but seems to have failed within 50 years, perhaps as a result of the Black Death. In 1679 the Thursday market was re-established and has continued ever since.
The market cross consists of a pedestal surmounted by a stone ball. It dates from 1756, but there was a significant restoration in 1896. The town hall dates to the 17th century, but a huge fire in the mid-18th century forced a substantial rebuild. The alleys, usually called weinds, were constructed so that each could be sealed off with stout gates whenever danger threatened.

 ⑥

From the market cross continue along the main road before turning right to pass the parish church of **St Thomas** on the way back to **Th'owd Tythe Barn**, which is indicated on the left.

13 Heysham

St Patrick's chapel, Heysham Head

The Walk 2$\frac{1}{2}$ miles. ⏱2 hours
Map: OS Landranger 97 Kendal & Morecambe (GR 410625)

How to get there

The village is around 3 miles (5 km) south-west of Morecambe. It can be reached by taking the A683 from Lancaster and then following the brown signs. Alternatively, there is a regular rail service to Morecambe from Lancaster and a bus service to the village. **Parking**: There is a large pay-and-display car park at the entrance to the village.

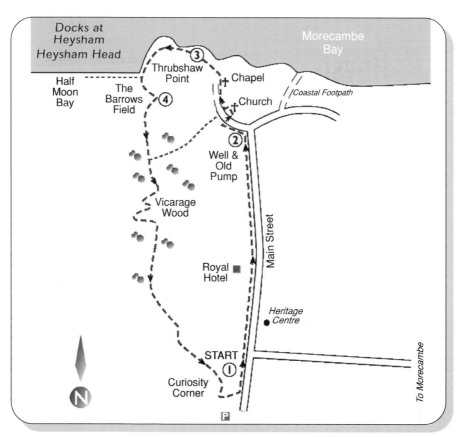

Introduction

Heysham is one of the most unspoiled villages in Britain. Its single street is lined with restaurants, cafes, 17th century cottages and a pub. The street leads down to the rocks of the shore and two ancient Christian sites. Then, it is on to Heysham Head, once the site of pleasure gardens and a carting circuit (which witnessed the early triumphs of a young Nigel Mansell), and now preserved as a nature area by the National Trust.

The Curiosity Corner Tea Rooms

From the car park my first stop is always at the Curiosity Corner Tea Rooms, a spotlessly clean place featuring home-made snacks and the local ice cream made by Bruciani. This Italian family have been 'Brits' since Victorian times. Here you can drink or buy bottles of nettle beer, a Heysham speciality, which goes down particularly well with a helping of Morecambe Bay shrimps. The

Drive and Stroll

Curiosity Corner serves breakfasts until 12 noon and closes at around 5 pm. Telephone: 01524 851902. Next door is a bistro which serves evening meals. Telephone: 01524 850500.

THE WALK

①

Begin at the **Curiosity Corner** and follow the main street. Look out for the Heritage Centre on the right.

The Heritage Centre is the place to find out about the history and natural history of Heysham. Formerly a barn serving the adjoining 17th century farmhouse, it is open free of charge and is staffed by local volunteers (telephone: 01524 859517). Books, local preserves, and memorabilia are on sale.

Continue along **Main Street**, looking out for the **Royal Hotel** on the left.

The Royal Hotel dates back to the 16th century and formerly functioned as a corn store. To the left of it is a cottage which was famous in the early 1900s for the nettle beer brewed there by Granny Hutchinson. Nettle beer is described as a tonic made from herbal extracts, sugar, yeast, lemons and, of course, nettles. It is said to stimulate the blood, help those who suffer from rheumatism, and also to be an 'unconfirmed' hair-restorer.

Just before the road forks, look for **St Patrick's Well**, also called the Church Well, on the left. It is set in an alcove and is reached by a set of steps.

The water is quite salty. Because of this, it was regarded as a cure, and pilgrims travelled long distances to drink it. Modern visitors are advised not to drink it and should stick to nettle beer.

②

Rejoin the street and fork left. On the right, on the opposite side of the road, is **St Peter's church**.

This is one of the most attractive and most ancient religious buildings in Lancashire. Heysham dates back to Saxon times and this church and St Patrick's chapel nearby were both established before the 8th century.

There is part of an Anglo-Saxon cross in the churchyard, and inside the church near the south door is a hog-back tombstone. Until 1961 it was in the churchyard but was brought indoors to prevent further erosion. Viking in origin, it dates to the 10th century. It is not unique but is the best example to be found anywhere in Britain. There are pagan symbols on one side and Christian signs on the other. Could this have marked the resting place of a Christian convert who felt like hedging his bets?

Curiosity Corner Tea Rooms

The view from the churchyard over Morecambe and its bay is wonderful and the panorama gets even better as a set of stone steps and a steep path lead on to Heysham Head.

St Patrick's Chapel was probably built in the late 8th century and extended in the 10th century. By the side of the chapel are some graves cut out of the solid rock. It is thought that the church and the chapel were part of an Irish religious settlement.

➌

Beyond the chapel, follow the track as it heads slightly left towards **Throbshaw Point**.

When the pleasure grounds closed in the 1960s it looked as if Heysham Head would become a housing estate. The National Trust, however, *bought the site and it is now a nature treasure house. A series of footpaths lead past bluebells, bugloss and other seaside flowers, and birdwatchers flock to the cliff edges to watch migratory and other movements with the ebb and flow of the tide. This area is thus a walk for all seasons.*

➍

Follow the path as it loops round to the left, away from the bay and round to **Barrows Field**, and from there climbs uphill to **Vicarage Wood**. Follow the winding footpath through the wood, on through an old orchard (where, according to the church register of 1753, plums, pears and apples once grew in 'profusion'), and finally down very steep stone steps back to the car park.

14 | Barrowford and Blacko

The old packhorse bridge, Higherford

The Walk 4 miles ⊕ 2½ hours
Map: OS Landranger 103 Blackburn & Burnley (GR 865398)

How to get there

Barrowford is a ribbon village, reached by turning off the M65 motorway at Junction 13. Take the second left turning off the junction and pass through the village along the A682. After passing the White Bear pub on the left look out for a right turn towards Colne. Pass an old tollhouse on the left and within a short distance turn sharp left into the Pendle Heritage Centre car park, where the walk starts. **Parking**: At Pendle Heritage Centre. There is no fee for parking but there is an honesty box for those who wish to help towards the upkeep.

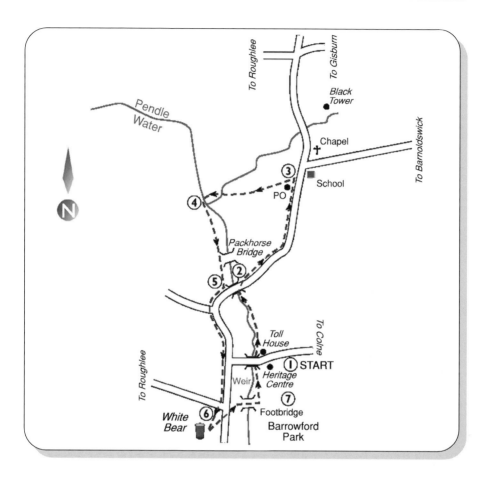

Introduction

This stroll passes through the heart of Barrowford, which grew during the start of the Industrial Revolution. After a climb up and over Blacko Hill the route drops down to a splendid river valley alongside a rippling brook and back into Barrowford.

The Pendle Heritage Centre

When Roger Bannister became the first man to run a sub four-minute mile few people realised that his ancestors were Lancastrians. The Bannister family home is now the Pendle Heritage Centre and dates to the 17th century.

Inside the centre itself is a shop selling books, local produce, and gifts mostly associated with the Pendle witch trials of 1612. This is the starting point of a long distance walk leading to Lancaster, where the witches were tried and executed. The centre is open daily. Telephone: 01282 661704.

The spacious café at the centre specialises in home prepared meals. I always enjoy not only the food but also the friendly atmosphere welcoming individuals and family groups alike. Meals, coffee and country tea and cakes are on offer, and there are good vegetarian options. One dining area overlooks the herb garden.

THE WALK

①

From the heritage centre car park find a signed footpath and follow **Pendle Water** upstream, keeping the river on the left.

②

Approach the main road towards **Gisburn** (A682). Look over to the left, where there is an old mill, now restored, which was once powered by a waterwheel. Cross the road and turn right across the bridge. The road climbs steeply through **Higherford** and into **Blacko**.

From the post office in Blacko two fascinating buildings are in view. To the right is the Methodist chapel where young Jimmy Clitheroe first performed when his accordion was taller than he was. By the 1950s the Clitheroe Kid was a household name. On the summit of Blacko Hill is Stansfields Tower. Some books state that this tower was once the home of Mother Demdike, one of the Lancashire witches, but it was actually a folly built by a grocer called Jonathan

Stansfield in 1891. He is said to have built the tower to raise the height of the hill so that he could see his girlfriend who lived in Gisburn. It can't have worked because they were never married.

From the post office turn left along a footpath signed **'Waters Meeting'**. The footpath descends steeply and follows the riverbank.

③

Cross a small bridge over the river and turn left. Pass an old tennis club on the right and continue into **Higherford**.

Pass a packhorse bridge on the left.

This recently restored structure is now used only by pedestrians. It is known locally as the Roman Bridge, although it dates from the 17th century. In 1748 the bridge was situated on what was then the main highway and John Wesley stood on it to preach his message. The vicar of Colne would not let Wesley enter his church and some locals were even more hostile, but he was given protection by John Hargreaves, a textile magnate.

Pendle Heritage Centre

Continue until the main road is reached and here turn right and follow the road to the **White Bear Inn**, which was the one-time home of John Hargreaves; parts of the building date back to Tudor times.

From the **White Bear** cross the main road and cross the river by an iron footbridge. This leads to **Barrowford Park**, which in the days of steam when lots of water was in demand was the site of a cotton mill and its associated lodge. The lodge is now a haven for wildfowl, especially in the winter.

Turn left and follow **Pendle Water**, looking down at the weir, which indicates that an earlier mill was water powered. This area is the haunt of dipper and grey wagtail. From the weir return to the heritage centre.

Look up to the right, where the holes in the wall indicate that pigeons were once kept for food for the Bannister family. Opposite the centre is a splendidly preserved tollhouse, which was built in 1803 and now forms part of the museum complex.

15 Ferndean and Wycoller

The old tannery lodge – a haven for wildlife

The Walk 6 miles ⏱3 hours
Map: OS Landranger 103 Blackburn & Burnley (GR 906399)

How to get there

From the M65 leave at the last junction (14). Follow the A6068 through North Valley Road, pass the Morris Dancers pub on the left and Colne Cricket Club on the right. Just after a roundabout turn right towards Trawden on the B6250. Look for Ball Grove picnic site, signed to the left, and, just before a bridge, the Cotton Tree pub on the left.
Parking: In the car park close to the Cotton Tree.

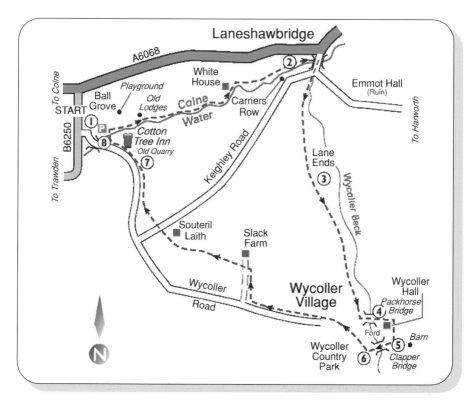

Introduction

This is one of my favourite walks because I was involved in its planning and was invited to perform the opening ceremony of the Ferndean Way.

The route takes in two country parks. Wycoller, once a centre of handloom weaving, was deserted when King Cotton was crowned and only recently has been reinhabited. It is now at the centre of the country park, and houses in the village are much sought after. In contrast to Wycoller, which has always been set in open countryside, Ball Grove Country Park was once a very smelly industrial site, now transformed into a riverside recreational area with a rich array of wildlife.

The Cotton Tree

This pub takes its name from a riverside area where the black poplar once grew. The species is a rarity these days and its old name was cotton tree, which well describes the appearance of its seed heads. Inside the pub is a date stone inscribed 1879, but its deeds suggest an earlier origin.

Drive and Stroll

In 2003 the Cotton Tree was extensively refurbished with the avowed intent of attracting walkers. Groups are welcomed with breakfast or tea and biscuits, at which time lunch can be ordered, thereby avoiding a wait at the conclusion of the walk. The menu is varied; local produce includes home-made steak pie and beef cobbler, which consists of a stew and dumplings. Families are welcome, and in summer there is a pleasant riverside beer garden.

On the beams are quotations, one of the most relevant being 'There is no love sincerer than love of food'. Telephone: 01282 863406.

THE WALK

①

Follow the path through the car park. Pass the weir and a concrete bridge. Keep to the left bank. Approach the top lodge and beyond this cross **Colne Water** by a wooden bridge. Climb a set of steps and follow an obvious flagged path. Pass two more bridges and then onto **Carriers Row** and **Laneshaw Bridge**.

②

Cross the **Keighley** road and find a stile on the opposite side. Cross this and follow the path alongside the stream. On the way to **Wycoller** the **Ferndean Way** and the 45-mile long **Pendle Way** footpaths converge. A look at the OS map will reveal that Colne Water becomes Wycoller Beck. In the background is **Boulsworth Hill**.

Cross a stile and look sharp left. In a wooded area in the distance is all that is left of **Emmot Hall**.

③

Cross two more stiles and turn left along a wall. Cross a stile which will challenge those who have a little excess weight to carry and then turn right. Two more stiles lead to a lane. Cross a bridge and turn left past **Lane Ends Farm**, which dates from the 17th century. Turn left into **Wycoller**.

④

Go over the packhorse bridge and approach **Wycoller Hall**. Although ruined, this building is still inspirational. Without doubt it was the model for Charlotte Brontë's Ferndean Manor in *Jane Eyre*. This is the end of the 3-mile long **Ferndean Way** and some walkers prefer to retrace their steps from here. This walk, however, has a different return route.

The area around **Wycoller Hall** is an ideal base from which to explore the country park. Look for the old crook barn, which serves as a museum devoted mainly to handloom weaving.

⑤

Returning from the barn, cross the clapper bridge. Turn right and pass through the village and bear left up the hill to the extensive car park.

Winewall

⤵ ⑥

From the car park turn left and keep to the right side of **Wycoller Road**. Look for the sign and follow the footpath towards **Slack Farm** on the right. Cross the road to **Slack Farm** and go over the stile in a wall to the right. Follow the edge of a field and cross another stile into a field. Head towards the farm buildings at **Souteril Laith**. Traverse a farmyard area and cross **Keighley Road**.

⤵ ⑦

Cross a wall stile close to a disused quarry and go through a gate which leads onto **Lane Top, Winewall**. Descend into **Winewall**, passing the **Cotton Tree Inn** on the right, and then cross the bridge over **Colne Water**. At the river turn right and follow the riverbank to **Ball Grove picnic site**.

The site now occupied by Ball Grove Country Park once housed one of the largest tanneries in Europe. It was set up by John and William Sagar in 1860, and at one time occupied an area of 8 acres and was worked by 300 men. Colne Water was used to power machinery and it was also needed in the tanning process itself. There were weirs and reservoirs which together provided 100,000 gallons of water per day.

The tannery operated until 1970, when it went bankrupt, and in 1974 demolition began. The reservoirs (known locally as lodges*) were retained. The lower lodge is now reserved for anglers whilst the higher lodge is an increasingly impressive wetland area, much loved by naturalists.*

16

Hollingworth Lake

Looking across Hollingworth Lake to the Promontory

The Walk 2½ miles ⏱2 hours
Map: OS Landranger 109 Manchester (GR 936146)

How to get there

From the M62 motorway leave at junction 21 and follow signs to Littleborough and then to Hollingworth Lake Country Park. The lake can also be reached from the A58, which links Halifax with Manchester. Follow the signs for the visitor centre. **Parking**: There is an extensive pay-and-display car park at the visitor centre.

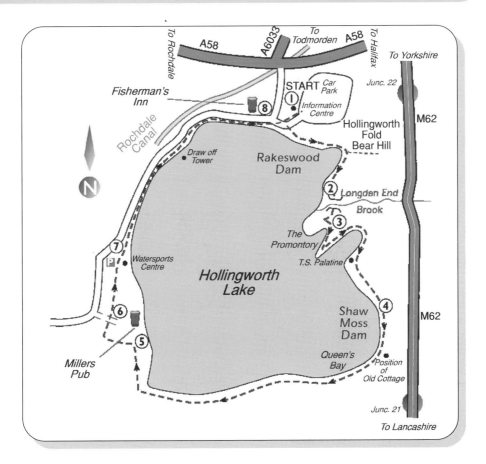

Introduction

This gentle circular stroll provides spectacular scenery over the Pennines to Blackstone Edge, which is 1550 feet (472 metres) above sea level. Here is one of the best preserved of the Roman roads to be found anywhere in Europe. Before the Romans there was a Bronze Age track over the hills – literally a 'high way' away from the wet and boggy valley. Soaring high above Hollingworth Lake is the M62, the modern equivalent of the ancient trans-Pennine route.

Hollingworth is not a natural stretch of water but a byproduct of the Rochdale Canal. The canal opened in 1804 and linked Sowerby Bridge with Manchester, a distance of 33 miles, and involved the construction of more than 90 locks. These needed water to operate, and the 'lake' was dug to provide this essential commodity.

Drive and Stroll

Mill workers used Hollingworth as a 'lung' and it became known as 'The Weyvers (weavers) Seaport'. It still has a seaside resort feel to it, and this makes the walk even more bracing. There can be no seaside resort that is as close to an ancient highway and a busy motorway (which from the lake looks surprisingly poetic).

The Millers

This pub and restaurant has a large car park. It offers a range of traditional dishes on its extensive menu, but it does, however, specialise in fish. There are outdoor tables and an impressive children's play area. On good days there is so much to see whilst enjoying a meal, as to the side is the base for the local sailing club and a training area for aspiring canoeists and wind surfers. Telephone: 01706 378163.

THE WALK

①

From the visitor centre proceed to the metalled road overlooking the lake.

The visitor centre has been the base of activities ever since the country park was created in 1974. There are displays, audiovisual presentations, an information point, a bookshop and an impressive little café. Telephone: 01706 373421.

Cross the road onto a promenade and turn left. This leads alongside the **Rakeswood Dam**. The area is popular with anglers all the year round, and day permits are available. Look out for an overflow, which is important in wet weather. This ensures that the lake never exceeds its capacity of 475 million gallons, which is one of the many reasons for Hollingworth's popularity throughout the year.

To the left is a turning to **Bear Hill** and close to is **Hollingworth Fold**, which until the mid 19th century was a toll road and evidence of the gates and other artefacts remain.

②

Cross a little footbridge over **Longden End Brook**, which is the main source of water for the lake.

On the bridge look out for a carved stone which reads RCN (Rochdale Canal Navigation). Here is an area set aside for wildlife; it has been developed following the silting up of a number of minor streams.

Follow the curve of the lake bank to the bird hide, which was erected in 1986. The area is a popular haunt for naturalists, with a variety of insects in summer and waterfowl throughout the year.

This leads on to The Promontory, which was a focal point in Victorian

The information centre at Hollingworth Lake

and Edwardian times and in the days of the Weavers' Seaport. The Lake Hotel has now gone, but at one time there was roller-skating, dancing, bowling, quoits and billiards. These days there is still a pavilion with toilets, a children's play area and a café.

♙ ③

From **The Promontory** follow the track, which bears right to T.S. Palatine. This is the headquarters for the local sea cadets and also a landing point for the *Lady Alice*, which is a small motor launch that ferries visitors around the lake.

♙ ④

Continue along the lakeside track

to the impressive **Shaw Moss Dam**, one of the three stout structures which resist the massive pressure built up by the water.

Nearby Queen's Bay is another reminder of Victorian times, when the Queen's Hotel was never short of clients. It was once a farmhouse called Peanock. Although it has long ceased to operate as a hotel, the building has not altered much. It is now called Queen's Cottage.

♙ ⑤

The track sweeps round to the right alongside the lake, and there are a number of wooden seats which are popular with picnickers.

Drive and Stroll

A left turn leads to **Millers pub and restaurant**.

✍ ⑥

Turn right to **Lane Bank Road**.

On the left are a number of cafés, restaurants, amusement arcades and gift shops which combine to produce a seaside atmosphere. To the right on the lake bank is a large pay-and-display car park and the water activities centre. This is open daily (telephone: 01706 370499).

There are large flocks of Canada geese and other waterfowl begging for food. Rowing boats can be hired by the hour, and here too is the main landing stage for the *Lady Alice*, which in the season takes up to about 40 passengers around the lake. This is worth a diversion; it takes about 25 minutes and adds another aspect to the sights on the stroll.

✍ ⑦

From the activity centre, near to which are toilets and a café, turn left and follow the obvious track beside the lake, passing the draw-off tower to the right.

In 1985 this was restored to bring the lake up to modern safety standards. It enables up to two million gallons of water to be drawn off each day to maintain the essential levels of the Rochdale Canal.

Continue along the track. The **Fisherman's Inn** to the left dates to 1800 and was once a farm. The car park is on the site of the stables, which were used for coach horses in the days of the toll road. The restaurant is known as **Wheavers**.

✍ ⑧

Face the **Fisherman's** and turn right. Cross the road, turn left, and return to the visitor centre and car park.

17 Haigh Hall Country Park

By the Leeds and Liverpool Canal

The Walk 6 miles ⏱3 hours
Map: OS Landranger 109 Manchester (GR 595088)

How to get there

Follow the brown signs from the M6 at junction 27 or from the M61 at junction 6. From Chorley and Standish use the A49. Haigh Hall is signed and reached by a track with traffic calmers. **Parking**: There is a large pay-and-display car park on the right (reasonable rates).

Drive and Stroll

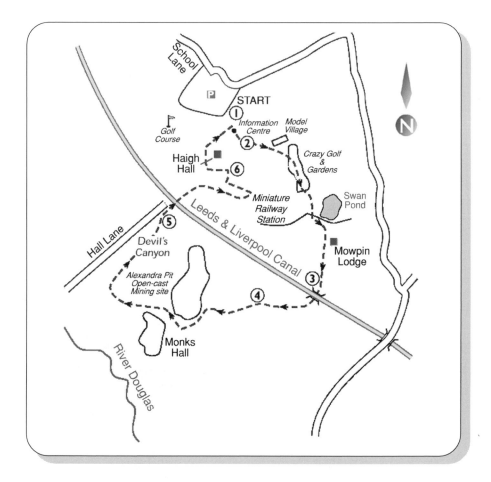

Introduction

For those who like to get their children interested in walking, this is a perfect route. Here is a mix of history and natural history, as well as a model village, a crazy golf course, an 18-hole golf course and a narrow gauge railway – enough to fill a whole day.

Young strollers will be entertained and should return home reasonably tired and exercised. For those beyond the first flush of youth there are splendidly beautiful gardens and scenic walks through well-signed trails. (Leaflets can be obtained detailing the history of the country park.) Throughout the walk there are views of the Leeds to Liverpool Canal; the route also runs close to the River Douglas.

The Haigh area was settled in Saxon times and the name literally means 'the enclosure'. The Bradshay family were on site from Norman times until 1770, when they ran out of male heirs. The estate then passed into the hands of ten-year-old Elizabeth Dalrymple, who ten years later married the Earl of Crawford. He was a shrewd businessman who used the coal and iron in the area to set up a foundry, reminders of which are found along the A49 road in the form of cast-iron mile markers, which are still in good repair.

Coal money also funded the replacement of the half-timbered hall. The new hall was constructed of stone between 1830 and 1849. In 1947 the house and 250 acre estate were bought by Wigan council and they now form one of the most impressive country parks in Britain.

The information centre and café at Haigh offers excellent food, which can be eaten in or out. The fare on offer is surprisingly varied. Telephone: 01942 832895.

The Crawford Arms

Nearby, on the road towards Standish, is the Crawford Arms, which has a large car park and is situated on the Leeds and Liverpool Canal. The food here is excellent and the canal outlook is a delight. Telephone: 01257 421313. There is also a good towpath walk, with plenty of boats to see and some good fishing.

THE WALK

①

From the car park pass the putting green on the right and nearby is the golf club and shop. To the left is a leisure centre. Turn left and left again through the arch leading to the old stable block, which houses the café, restaurant, shop and information centre.

②

Return through the arch, bear left, and follow the wide track, passing the model village and crazy golf course. Pass through a gate into a delightful garden which has a number of seats ideal for picnics.

Continue towards an area known as the **Swan Pond**, which in summer is full of water plants, dragonflies and butterflies. In winter the area is of interest to birdwatchers.

The path bears right at **Mowpin Lodge**, continues along the well-made track, and passes the narrow gauge railway. This is an ideal place for young people to enjoy a train journey and to explore the mature woodlands from the track.

③

The route then leads down to the **Leeds to Liverpool Canal**. Turn right here and follow the towpath to the next bridge.

Drive and Stroll

The Crawford Arms

 ④

Turn left along a wooded path, passing the former Alexandra open cast mining site on the right, evidence that the Haigh area was once a major coal producing area.

In 1653 Sir Roger Brandshaigh built a sough or drainage ditch. Following the closure of a number of small pits in the 19th and 20th centuries, red iron salts began to seep through the ground and discolour the water. The Yellow Brook has since been well named.

The Haigh sough is set to undergo improvements beginning in 2004, and the coal authority and the Environment Agency are combining to improve the water quality. Eventually an extensive wetland area will be produced, which will greatly enhance this already attractive stroll.

Follow a sweeping loop that leads to **Monks Hill**. The name would seem to indicate that there was once a monastic interest here. The Haigh coal is of a type called cannel, which is so full of carbon that it burns almost without smoke. It is so 'pure' that it can also be polished and used to produce ornaments.

Keep bearing left as the path leads into an area known as **Devil's Canyon**, which has become an increasingly important rock climbing area.

🥾 ⑤

Keep bearing right until the path diverges. Take a sharp left turn and follow the track to the canal bridge. Cross the bridge and follow the obvious path, later passing the miniature railway on the right.

Carry straight on along the wide drive up to **Haigh Hall**.

The hall is not open to the general public but is a popular conference centre and a delightful and popular spot to hold a wedding reception.

Approach the front of the hall and then bear left and right along the side of the building. There are seats on the left which overlook the golf course, and this is another ideal place to have a rest and enjoy a picnic.

🥾 ⑥

Turn right and then left. A steep climb leads to the information centre on the right. Continue straight ahead and then left into the car park.

18 | Bury to Ramsbottom

Summerseat Station

The Walk 4 miles ⏱2 hours
Map: OS Landranger 109 Manchester – GR 795110 starting from Bury;
GR 793168 starting from Ramsbottom

How to get there

For Bury (Bolton Street Station) follow the M66 motorway and leave at junction 2. Follow the signs towards Bury and then the brown signs indicating East Lancashire Railway. The starting point can also be reached from the A56. Alternatively, to start from Ramsbottom and do the walk in reverse, take the M66 and at junction 1 turn off onto the A56 and down to the well-marked station. **Parking**: For Bury, there is a pay and display car park opposite the station. For Ramsbottom, cross the railway crossing and turn immediately left to the extensive car park.

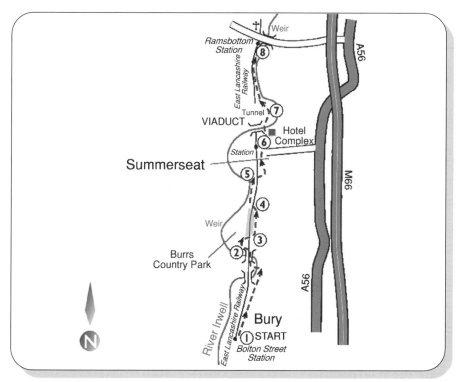

Introduction

This is a linear walk and can be followed in either direction. The return journey can be made on the steam railway.

This walk winds its way alongside the railway line and the majestic meanderings of the Irwell, now noted as one of the most improved rivers in Europe.

The East Lancashire Railway runs from Wednesday to Sunday during the summer and also on most winter weekends. (For running details ring 0161 7647790.) Timetables are available from Bury, Ramsbottom and Rawtenstall stations and from local tourist information offices.

Anyone wishing to follow the Irwell Valley Way will find the railway ideal, and in 2004 the line will be extended from Bury to Heywood, adding an extra four miles.

The Trackside

This pub on Bury's East Lancashire Railway platform is a pub with a difference. It has been adapted without too many alterations from the old

Drive and Stroll

station buffet and captures a feeling of the 1940s. The buffet bar, however, is of a much earlier vintage, the station complex dating back to the 1850s.

The Trackside specialises in a very wide selection of real ales. The hand pumps are a feature; and there is also a wide selection of bottled beers, ciders, and malt whisky. Those of us who drive and stroll cannot afford to sample all on offer. However, tea and coffee are also served, and there is an interesting menu, including the famous Bury Black Pudding, served with mustard and piccalilli, and Isle of Man kippers. Telephone: 0161 764779.

THE WALK

①

At **Bolton Street station** enjoy what the East Lancashire Railway has on offer and then turn left and cross the **Castlecroft Road**. The route then passes under **Castlecroft Road**, crosses over the river Irwell, and continues along the **Peel Walk** footpath; this follows an old railway track which at one time led towards **Holcombe**.

②

Turn right into **Woodhill Road** and then go on into **Burrs Country Park**. This has become very popular since the **Irwell** is now a much cleaner river. At this point the route lies between the river on the left and the railway on the right. A weir here is much frequented by canoeists who travel from miles away to learn the essential techniques of negotiating white water. There are lots of winding tracks alongside the river and it is worth exploring these even if it adds an extra half mile or so to the journey.

③

The track veers away from the river and passes under the railway via a bridge. Pass **Springside Farm** on the right and carry on for $1/4$ mile. Turn left and follow the track along the margin of a field.

④

Look for a railway cutting on the left. Descend to the railway and cross the line, obeying the warnings and crossing the line with great care. Look out for the river Irwell below on the left.

⑤

Approach a road, turn right, and cross under the railway bridge. Turn left and head for **Summerseat Station**.

Summerseat (its name is from Old Norse and denotes a summer shelter or shieling) is a delightful village which once made its living from cotton. The early mills were converted water mills, the Irwell having provided the source of power, with steam coming later.

⑥

Follow the track from the station to

The view from Summerseat Station

the **Waterside Hotel and Restaurant**, set on the banks of the Irwell. This was once a huge cotton mill, which has recently been converted into up-market residences and a hotel.

Continue from the **Waterside** and cross the **Irwell**. Bear left and pass beneath the majestic railway viaduct, which is still in use. At the end of a line of old cottages turn right and climb an incline which follows a cobbled path.

↳ ⑦

Cross the railway close to the entrance to a tunnel. Ascend the path, bearing left, and look out for the railway track as it emerges from the tunnel and then enters a cutting. Turn right and then descend to the left, ensuring that the **Irwell** is on the right.

↳ ⑧

Cross the **Irwell** for the last time on this walk. Pass through a pleasant park and turn left on the main road to arrive at **Ramsbottom Station**.

Dominating the hill around Ramsbottom and Holcombe is the Peel Tower. The tower is 128 feet high, and there is a well-marked but quite strenuous walk up from Ramsbottom station.

This recently restored monument was erected in 1852 to celebrate the life of Sir Robert Peel (1788–1850), the Bury lad who became Prime Minister in the 1840s. He set up the first police force, hence the colloquial terms Peelers and Bobbies for policemen.

Return to **Bury Station** by the East Lancashire Railway steam train service. Look to the left as you approach the viaduct; the views down to the **Waterside** are magnificent.

19 Burscough Priory and Lathom Chapel

Lathom chapel and almshouses

The Walk 4 miles ⏱2 hours
Map: OS Landranger 108 Liverpool (GR 431105)

How to get there

Follow the A59 from Preston towards Liverpool and find the Bull and Dog Inn on the right between Ormskirk and Burscough. Alternatively, leave the M6 motorway at junction 27. Take the A5209, passing through Parbold to Burscough. Turn left and find the Bull and Dog on the right. The nearest railway stations are at Ormskirk and Burscough junction, and there is a regular bus service between Ormskirk and Burscough that runs past the Bull and Dog, which is about half way (1½ miles) between these stations. **Parking**: The pub has an extensive car park.

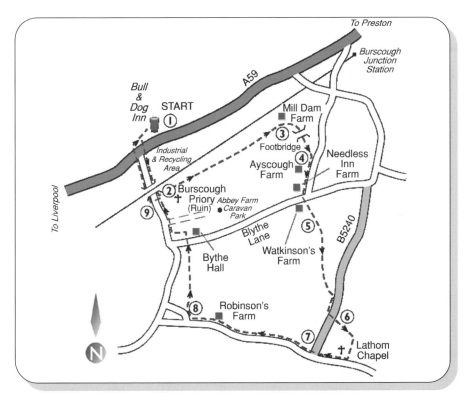

Introduction

This is a majestic and historic stroll linking Burscough Priory and Lathom chapel. The route leads through gloriously beautiful countryside. Around Lathom there are still signs of the severe damage caused during the First Civil War. Those who think that the conflict between Charles I and Cromwell did not have much impact on old Lancashire will have cause to think again when they stroll along this route! Walkers should be aware that the route crosses a major railway line, and great care should be taken, especially by those who are accompanied by children or dogs.

The Bull and Dog

This pub has catered for visitors since the coaching days of the 18th and 19th centuries. This is the place to build up strength prior to the walk or replace lost energy on return. Why not do both by enjoying a pre-walk coffee and a meal at the end? The menu is varied and usually includes local produce. Telephone: 01704 894418.

Drive and Stroll

THE WALK

①

From the **Bull and Dog** cross the busy road with care. Go down a road into an area dominated by an industrial site and a recycling centre. Leave this on the left and take care as you go towards and then cross the railway line.

Look out to the left for the ruins of **Burscough Priory** which is now on private land and set around a farm. There is a good view from the track revealing the Augustinian priory, which was founded in 1189.

The priory was never large and at the dissolution of the monasteries there were just the prior and four monks in residence. Although only a few traces of the priory remain, what is left has a haunting feel to it. The bells of the priory now ring out from the tower of Ormskirk church, which until the dissolution had just a spire. The tower was added to house the monastery bells, although legend has it that the spire and the tower were built on the separate instructions of two eccentric sisters who had been unable to agree as to which the church should have.

②

Turn left through a field and cross a footbridge to approach **Mill Dam Farm** to the left; the name suggests that the monks once had a watermill here to grind flour.

③

Bear very slightly left up a track, thus avoiding the farm, and then turn right and cross a series of well-maintained stiles before reaching a farm track.

④

Turn right and cross a concrete footbridge. Pass a group of houses and cross a road to a farm track. Pass between the buildings of **Ayscough Farm** and continue along an obvious path through fields towards **Needless Inn Farm**.

⑤

By **Watkinson's Farm** ignore the main farm track and follow a less obvious but still well marked track. Keep a belt of trees to the right. Cross a footbridge and turn right onto a minor road.

⑥

Find a clear sign indicating **Lathom** and follow this to some almshouses and a chapel. This is all that remains of **Lathom House**, which was a power base of the Royalist Stanleys, whose head was the Earl of Derby. Their main house was destroyed following civil war sieges in 1644 and 1645. The site is now part of Pilkington's St Helen's glass research.

Lathom Park chapel was built in 1500 and dedicated to St John the Divine. A close look at the furnishings will reveal a lectern and

Cromwell's stone

screen which were brought from Burscough Priory following its dissolution. The screen has bullet marks on it, suggesting that the Roundhead troops had no respect for the sanctity of the chapel. There is also a large stone with hollows in it into which molten lead was poured to produce cannon balls. These are still being dug up around the old house, which was the target of Parliamentarian troops.

 ⑦

From the chapel turn right and follow the road beside a golf course.

 ⑧

Pass **Robinson's Farm** and turn right into **Blythe Lane**. Cross a stile into a field and enjoy the views of **Blythe Hall**, which is privately owned and still moated. This site

has been occupied since Norman times and possibly even earlier.

At one time Blythe Hall was owned by Lord Skelmersdale and his famous guests included Ivor Novello and Noel Coward.

Turn left near the hall in the direction of **Abbey Farm caravan site** and a sign indicating a private road. Use is restricted to vehicles visiting the caravan park but the route is an official footpath. The owners of the caravan park are very welcoming and many people bring caravans and tents for use as a base for walking.

 ⑨

Follow the track towards the railway, crossing the lines with care, and continue along the road to return to the **Bull and Dog** on the other side of the A59.

20 | Around Rufford

Rufford Old Hall from the gardens

The Walk 3½ miles ⏱2½ hours but allow an extra 2 hours to explore the hall and gardens.
Map: OS Landranger 108 Liverpool (GR 464161)

How to get there

From Preston follow the A59 towards Liverpool and follow the signs for Rufford, which is astride this road. Alternatively, leave the M6 motorway at junction 27 and follow the A5209 to Parbold. From Parbold follow the B5246 to Rufford. **Parking**: There is parking at the railway station and at Rufford Old Hall, where this walk begins.

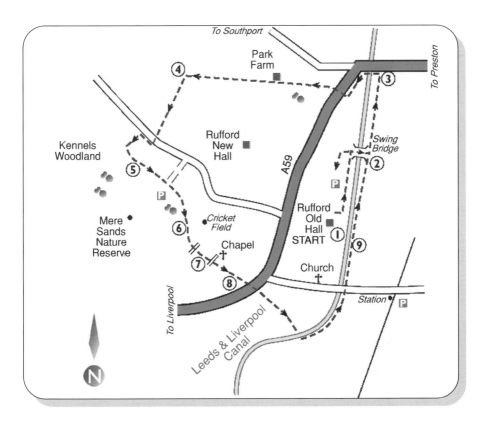

Introduction

There are few more contrasting walks than this. It leads from a historic hall along a canal towpath and through farmland and a nature reserve with a good population of healthy red squirrels and a wintering population of wildfowl which would be hard to beat anywhere in the county.

Rufford Old Hall is sandwiched between a branch of the Leeds and Liverpool Canal and the A59. The $14\frac{1}{2}$ acres of grounds have been National Trust property since 1936. This historic spot breathes tranquillity, and there is a welcoming feel to the place. On cold days open fires crackle in the grates and visitors can sit and soak up the heat. If the mood takes you, you can even play the piano, but on some days a professional pianist performs. Rufford has been used to having skilled entertainers on site since it was built by the Hesketh family in the mid 16th century. It has been proved beyond doubt that the family employed a theatre company a member of which was the

Drive and Stroll

young William Shakespeare. And those who love architecture will marvel at the great hall with its hammer beam roof dating from 1485.

The hall is open from Easter to Christmas. Throughout 2004 it will be open on Sundays, when a traditional Lancashire lunch will be served. Rufford Hall is aiming to attract more and more visitors and hoping that many will enjoy return visits and the food. Both traditionally attired visitors and walkers are welcome. Telephone: Ruffold Old Hall 01704 823811; the café 01704 821254. You can also visit the National Trust web site (www.nationaltrust.org.uk).

The Old Kitchen Restaurant

This establishment serves teas and meals in the original kitchen, complete with its open fire. Most of the food is carefully produced on site, and wherever possible local produce is used. It is open from 11 am for morning coffee; lunches are served from 12 noon to 2 pm and afternoon teas until 5 pm.

THE WALK

I always begin this walk in the old stable yard of Rufford Old Hall. Nearby are good toilet facilities, the restaurant, the shop, and the splendid Philip Ashcroft Museum. This is housed in the old washhouse and displays local country artefacts. Philip Ashcroft gave his collection to the National Trust before his untimely death in 1959 at the age of 46.

①

1. From the old stable block turn right through the car park and along the woodland footpath which keeps the canal on the right. This leads out into fields.

②

At a swing bridge over the canal turn right and immediately left. Continue parallel with the canal to the **Spark Road** bridge.

③

Pass beneath the bridge and go up the wooden steps onto the road, turning left over the canal, and then left again. Follow the towpath and turn over the A59 into **Spark Road.** On the opposite side of the road there will be a bridleway called **Croston Drive**. Look out for woodland on the left and beyond the trees **Rufford New Hall**.

The 18th century was a period of dissatisfaction when many landed gentry felt their half-timbered houses were too humble. The Heskeths built their new hall in 1788, but of the two the older building has stood the test of time much better.

The fly agaric toadstool can be seen along the way

The new hall has recently been the subject of a large restoration programme and building development. Some of the ambience of the building, which is not open to the public, does remain, however.

Follow a wide track beside the outbuildings of Park Farm and continue to a junction.

④

Here continue straight ahead along a wide track, passing a knot of trees and a pond. Continue as the track widens. Where it meets a minor road, turn right, cross the road, and look for a signpost. Follow the route of the path along a field and across a footbridge and follow the most obvious track, which lies close to a boarding kennels, to reach **Mere Sands Wood**.

Mere Sands Wood Nature Reserve is owned and managed by the local wildlife trust. The reserve covers 105 acres (42 hectares) of broadleaf and conifer woodland, lakes, and heathland. From 1974 to 1982 the site was a sand quarry, valuable because it was used to produce high quality glass. Following its closure, ponds were landscaped, a splendid visitors' centre constructed, bird hides built, and footpaths laid out. In winter the ponds are frequented by

Drive and Stroll

wildfowl and waders, and in the summer the woodlands provide an ideal breeding place for more than 50 species of bird.

Entry is free and it is worth extending this walk by exploring the area, which is the haunt of red squirrels, very much a rarity in England these days.

Close to the car park a well marked footpath follows a woodland edge, in which a variety of fungi can be seen in autumn. Telephone: 01704 821809.

⑤

Cross a stile and bear left. Turn left again, coming out of the wooded area close to a little stream. Look out for Rufford's impressive cricket ground on the left. Emerge onto a narrow road.

⑥

Near a bridge look for a signpost and follow the twisting path as indicated, passing close to an old Methodist chapel, which is now used as a retreat and small conference centre.

Turn right across another bridge and then left through a farmyard. Look for a gap and a stream.

Follow this route until the A59 is reached.

⑦

Ascend to the bridge and cross over the road and then turn left to a swing bridge over the canal.

The canal was constructed in 1781 by the Leeds and Liverpool Canal Company as a north-south link. This connected the main canal at Burscough (2 miles south of Rufford) to the navigable lower reaches of the River Douglas, which is 4 miles to the north near Tarleton. This in turn reaches the sea via the Ribble estuary.

⑧

Follow the delightful towpath, passing the railway station and car park to the right. Follow the canal bank and pass **St Peter's church** and **Rufford Old Hall** on the left. This wooded towpath is another area brimming with wildlife.

Continue to the swing bridge; turn left over the bridge and then immediately left again to return to the car park at the Old Hall.